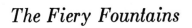

The Fiery Fountains

By Margaret Anderson

MY THIRTY YEARS' WAR
THE FIERY FOUNTAINS
THE LITTLE REVIEW ANTHOLOGY
THE UNKNOWABLE GURDJIEFF
THE STRANGE NECESSITY

The old fiery fountains are far off.
—WILLIAM BUTLER YEATS

MARGARET ANDERSON

The Fiery Fountains

THE AUTOBIOGRAPHY

continuation and crisis to 1950

HORIZON PRESS   NEW YORK

FOR

FIVE

FRIENDS

Margaret Anderson was one of the great figures in the period from 1914 to 1929, the period that is sometimes thought of as a minor American renascence.

What are the words to describe those years? Not "Jazz Age," not "The Roaring Twenties," not "Flaming Youth" —these are cheap labels for certain surface phenomena. They do not even hint that this decade and a half was a time of rebellion and expectancy, of search and promise, of creative expansion and electric vitality.

It did not seem to matter to us then that political America, after the defeat of Woodrow Wilson, belonged to the conservatives typified by Coolidge and Hoover. It didn't matter because outside of politics the tone was set by the New.

Industry left the Machine Age and entered the new Power Age. New York City became a world capital. New ideas in physics and psychology woke up the young. Everywhere one looked the new appeared—in education, it was "progressive education"; in the theatre, it was the "little theatre movement"; in the magazine world, it was the *New Republic*, the revitalized *Dial*, and later the *New Yorker* and *Time*; in book publishing, it was new firms with revolutionary promotion methods. And there were the new writers here and abroad: in poetry, Frost, Eliot, Pound, Stevens, Williams, Crane; in prose, Hemingway, Sherwood Anderson, Fitzgerald, Joyce, Wyndham Lewis, Proust . . . the list could run on and on.

Most of the writers I have named appeared in the magazine Margaret Anderson founded and edited—*The Little Review*. Here was concentrated the essence of the period: the New.

In *My Thirty Years' War*, the first volume of her autobiography, Margaret Anderson told about her rebellious youth. Born in Indianapolis, and growing up in a social milieu pointed toward country club standards, she revolted against this environment by the time she reached Western College at Oxford, Ohio. She packed up and went to Chicago, then a center of literary rebellion. She wanted to be free.

It was a time of rebels but it was observed of many of them that they were more concerned in becoming free *from* something than in being free *for* something. I think that this could be said of fiery Emma Goldman who in those early Chicago years impressed Margaret Anderson. Emma Goldman was a great reactor against what she conceived to be fetters on the human spirit but her positive goals were nebulous. Margaret Anderson was positive. Her negations were only by-products of a passionate search for freedom-as-fulfilment.

If you would feel that restless, excited, impassioned search, turn over the file of *The Little Review*, now a collector's prize. Freedom-as-fulfilment was to be found in the arts, Margaret Anderson appears to have reasoned, but she did not find it there. She found something else—great expressions of vitality: the singing of Mary Garden, the painting of Joseph Stella, the experimentation of James Joyce, the critical notes of Ezra Pound.

In those days the younger generation read *The Little Review* from cover to cover, not missing a word of the advertisements, and Margaret Anderson was their goddess of the arts.

In 1924 Margaret Anderson's search for an unimaginable freedom went beyond the arts, and the present volume tells about her journey to the "old fiery fountains," the source of great living which feeds art, religion, science and philosophy. In this book there comes to the surface again the exploring spirit that distinguished the Twenties, and that in some figures of the Twenties, including notably Margaret Anderson, never diminished.

GORHAM MUNSON

A PARTIAL PORTRAIT
by Janet Flanner

Since her early twenties, Margaret Anderson has been a romantic, *in situ*, and a functioning active rebel. As a literary rebel she was less interested in devaluing what was old and outworn in writing than in the discovery of what was new and valid in its proof of the imperative miracle of change on which she based her career as the founder and editor of the *Little Review*. The greater part of her long life has been structured on her wide and superior enthusiasm for what was new in American and English writing in our time, —words in the service of the communication of what she felt in the early days was close to some absolute in modern writing, close to what was perfected whether in prose or poetry, to what was intimate with the rare and even with the inspired in the way of thinking and feeling, and in the way of imagining and of summing-up, all of it condensed within that literate human miracle which is vocabulary. As a rebel, her rebellion consisted functionally of her appreciation for what only a few writers were then writing in special ways and that few readers wished to read. Organization being to her what she called "the elixir of stimulation," without hesitation she took over the task in the *Little Review*, (later shared by Jane Heap), of organizing a new kind of reader-appreciation in the United States, first in Chicago, then in New York and occasionally in California, the geographic fragments of America where her magazine fought (mostly against lack of regular funds) for its survival and its increasing influence and value. Part of her equipment as an editor of what was new was that she was a kind of touch-stone in her literary taste. As time went on she expanded this to her belief that her taste was infallible, which was almost equally true. Her autocracy was tempered by her insatiable curiosity to hear the other person's point of view in disagreement with her own, since argument as explanation was her delight and in conversation could last literally from dusk to dawn. Lawless by nature, she always practised a variety of polite anarchy as her basis of conduct. Her romanticism could be described as her passionate desire for the creation and maintenance of an art of life, and its emotions, to the aesthetic in the art of painting or of sculpture—an art of living, an art of human relations, beginning with one's relation to one's self. Her sense of physical elegance was something special, like a form of personal pleasure, that was very becoming to her beautiful face and exquisite large hands on which in her heyday in Greenwich Village she invariably wore white gloves. That is to say, she always wore the right white glove and removed the left white glove so that she could hold her lighted cigarette in her favorite hand which was her left.

x

Then through absent-mindedness she usually lost the left-hand glove. However, as she was a stickler in matters of appearance, no matter how empty her purse, she usually carried clasped in her right hand another glove, folded, which was a relict of a previous pair, but fulfilled the function of seeming to substitute for what she had lost. In my memory, the two white gloves remain over years as a touching inanimate portion of her portrait.

Of her two autobiographical volumes, *The Fiery Fountains,* published in 1951, which is the second, is the one which her oldest friends are most gratified to see reprinted now, so that what it contained can be more widely savoured today. It covers and explores the most enriching two decades of her life, animated by the long consummately felicitous personal friendship with Madame Georgette Leblanc, who had earlier been the wife of Maeterlinck. The second enrichment had been their search together in the cosmological philosophy of Gurdjieff for some new illumination to bring to living, a study then centered in his classes in Fontainebleau-Avon where he had founded his Institute for the Harmonious Development of Man, housed in a fine old priory where for a time the two friends lived.

It is in *The Fiery Fountains* that Margaret Anderson became an invaluable writer on the emotions, on objective love, on superior romantic love, on amity, on perfections in friendship, on civilizing love for nature, for trees whose names she did not even know, for sun and rain and for the moon in the evening sky. In all that she wrote Georgette Leblanc became an inhabitant. Shortly before the war began

Margaret knew that Georgette Leblanc was doomed, that the operation she had survived could not save her. It was ten years later that *The Fiery Fountains* was first published. With Margaret's editorial habit she had filed a letter I wrote to her when I first read her book, a letter she has now sent back to me. In it I had written in part, "That you have preserved yourself in words makes an invaluable record, for you have to be read to be believed. Futhermore, to make readers actually believe in the existence of love is the hardest task for a writer. In your book through your sensibilities and their weight you establish the reality of love as a *fact*. You gain a remarkable concentrated personal quality in your report of all you touch upon or list and on this accumulation a landscape line, as it were, is achieved, with variations in it which keep the reader gazing at what you tell as it moves uphill to its high point of loss and tragedy,"—in her friend Georgette's death.

May 15, 1969

CONTENTS

1. LANDSCAPE
with Figures

1. LANDSCAPE

with Figures

Once upon a time, many years ago, when I was living happily ever after . . .

It was in France, in Tancarville, Normandy, in a lighthouse—not one of those stern and formal lighthouses on a rocky coast, but a small friendly whitewashed house that looked rather like a country church. It stood on a white cliff, with a river in front of it and a forest behind.

We lived in the lighthouse through spring, summer and autumn, and since we loved it above all other places we would have stayed on through winter if we could have kept warm. We tried to buy it but it wasn't for sale, so we rented it . . . for fifty francs a month.

Petunias grew around the doorstep—pink and mauve and red. Hollyhocks, sweetpeas and tobacco flowers filled the garden, magenta phlox grew against white walls. Before the end of February primroses and violets bloomed among dead leaves. I was never quite able to decide which of the seven seasons I loved most at the lighthouse—the two springs, summer, the three autumns, or winter. I never spent a winter in this changing place but once I went for an afternoon, night and morning in December and almost decided that winter was best. Perhaps this was because of my mood, which was stripped like the landscape. I remember there was only one leaf left on the maple tree and I watched it in the afternoon wind, wondering if it would be there in the morning. During the night snow fell. When I looked out at the leaf again it was still on its branch, sprinkled with white.

But perhaps September was my favorite time. September in Normandy is a slow dream; mists overhang the night and in the hours that precede morning, fog bells clang along the river banks like bells ringing in the earth. By nine the mists have risen; by noon a stationary sun holds life in perspective, by six o'clock it has become a pink balloon floating on the horizon—you can look at it directly as at the moon. Then evening mists mount in the valleys and lie all night upon the fields.

At the top of the lighthouse there was a tower. A hundred years ago its light had swept over wide waters below, for the sea came up to the foot of the cliffs where the Seine now flows. There had been no light in the tower for many years. In its glass dome we had put a window-seat from which we could survey the country. To the west, fifteen miles away, were Le Havre and the sea; to the east the château where we sometimes spent the winter. There was no house within sight or sound—nothing but sky, water, trees and, across the river, fields with cows. During the day boats passed on the Seine, flying the flags of all the nations of the world; at night the lights from Port Jerome, to the southeast, made of the far coast a riviera. All through the night long barges slipped by on the dark waters beneath our windows; we knew they were coming by the faint drum of their motors as they turned the bend of the river, where the château stands facing the sandbar. Once a month at midnight, when the moon was full, a lighted pleasure boat floated by. From its deck a waltz reached up to our windows and found us standing there, motionless, in our dream.

So, my landscape is France—a country I never think of as a nation but as a place of soft sun, thin rain, hazel light, russet earth, olive-green rivers, tawny trees, white roads, scarlet poppies—a place where you would like to live forever, in an eternal recurrence, as if you were living the life of a field.

In my landscape there are three figures, and a shadowed fourth who chose the background. The first is Jane Heap. I tried to describe her and her remarkability in a book I wrote in 1930, *My Thirty Years' War;* I shall let her speak for herself in this one. What did she look like? Handsome features, strongly cut, rather like those of Oscar Wilde in his only beautiful photograph; but when Jane talked you were conscious of only one feature—her soft deep eyes, in which you could watch thought take form . . . thought that was always clearest when she talked of the indefinable, the vast, or the unknown; thought that made other people's thinking seem unnecessary.

In 1914, in Chicago, I had founded the *Little Review,*

5

a magazine of the arts "making no compromise with the public taste." Later Jane became co-editor and we moved the magazine to New York where we tried in vain to convince Anthony Comstock and three judges that James Joyce's *Ulysses*, which we were publishing serially, was the literary masterpiece of our generation. Time proved us right, but in 1918 we were tried and convicted of printing "obscene literature." Jane and I were fined and had our fingerprints taken in the Federal court of New York where we are still classified, I suppose, as criminals.

The principal figure in my landscape is a person who, to anyone who knew her, is identified with whatsoever things are perfect—Georgette Leblanc. She had come to America in 1920, after her separation from Maeterlinck, to renew her life in a new world. Describe her? Jean Cocteau said this: "Georgette was the model for a lyric saint—one of those strange great beings who move through the crowd, headless and armless, propelled only by the power of their souls, as immutable as the Victory of Samothrace." What did she look like? I have seen strangers stop her and say, "You have the most beautiful face in the world." It was an art face. A sculptor trying to draw it said of her eyebrows and arch of forehead, *"C'est le Parthénon."*

We cannot have met by chance, Georgette and I, since we knew at once that we were to join hands and advance through life together. Ah, I said, when I first saw her marvelous mystic face: this is the land I have been seeking; I left home long ago to discover it—a new continent, an unearthly place, the great world of art; not a personal but a classical world—formal, magical, mythical. At first I could not understand her language, but when I did I was not surprised to discover that she always said the matchless thing. For twenty years I listened to her words, always with the feeling that I was being blessed or rescued. Ah, I continued to say for the rest of my life.

The figure always in the background, but always indispensable to the landscape and atmosphere, is Monique. Thirty years before this story she had been a schoolteacher in Brussels and had heard Georgette sing "Thaïs" at the Opéra de la Monnaie. Her first gesture afterward was to buy a bunch of violets and put it on Thaïs's doorstep. For nearly fifty years, altogether, Monique was to offer violets in every way she could devise, from cooking to teaching; she had a degree in science and could instruct Georgette in those rudiments which such a pupil would never have the patience to learn for herself. Georgette called her "a fairy-tale nurse, a character met only in books with colored illustrations, a nature without an angle, a being whose words and steps make no sound and who always offers to agree with me."

We three lived in France. Jane lived in England.

We spent our eternal summers at the lighthouse in a kind of incredulous delight, loving France above all other countries and loving each other above all others.

From the beginning, I remember, I knew that life in France would be what life should be, or at least that I could live life there as it should be lived. This I did for twenty years, and to me those years were as different from

7

life in other places as a flower is from a seed. They were the happiest years of a too-happy life. Merely to remember them is to be convinced that no one ever lived a venture so complete in self-intoxication. We accomplished the great interdiction—that of ignoring the world for our world—with full consciousness of what we were doing and much confidence that we were not merely producing a lovely disaster. France allowed us to live our secret formulas. It is an impersonal country where everyone is free to establish his personal heaven on earth.

At this time we had less money than anyone in the world (including those who have none at all), but we spent twenty years in five of the more celestial French châteaux. Two of them were *monuments historiques*—one had been built by François Premier and lived in by Louis XV and Louis XVI; the other—the château de Tancarville—had sheltered Richard Coeur de Lion and Elizabeth of England. The third had belonged to Madame de Maintenon; the fourth, in Neuilly, had been a *pied-à-terre* of Louis XIV; and the fifth, in St. Germain-en-Laye, a *pied-à-terre* of Napoleon. Besides these elysian abodes we also dwelt in the more heavenly hotels and houses, inns and abbeys, peasant-huts and hunting-lodges, mountain hamlets and fishing villages . . . and always the luminous lighthouse.

Of course there were times when we were not sure of surviving, when no reasonable being would have granted us the least chance of survival; there were months when it was difficult even to find fifty francs for lighthouse rent; there were moments when we speculated that suicide would be our best solution. We realized that we were anachronisms—to live for art was no longer quite *àpropos*. In the world outside us the era of personal exaltation had waned. Georgette had to admit the fact of energies without issue— meaning frustration; I had to admit the fact of emotions without issue—meaning incompetence; Monique, who lived to help us conceal both facts, had to admit failure. But we always lived our version of the old fiery fountains. We had come to middle years, but we never had the corresponding emotions; our years had a quality that depends not on youth but on species—the quality of life as against non-life. By which I mean: an obsession with wonder and delight.

Though Georgette was twenty years older than I, we never thought of this fact at all. We lived, always, as people do sometimes: as after a shock, a loss, or a revelation, when one is more accessible to the great emotions. Because we lived like this in France, that country became our fountain of eternal years.

To define the real beneficence of France you cannot avoid the over-used word "light." The light you are so conscious of on rivers, gardens, boulevards, squares, courtyards, cathedrals and fields, seems also to fall upon your spirit. In France I always felt that I could accomplish anything, lightly, under conditions that would always remain, no matter how long I procrastinated, ideal.

In France you need not, today, think of tomorrow— you can celebrate today. You have time for the seasons, you can identify with them slowly, as you drink good wine. In the country you can feel like the peasants in

Millet's "Angelus," in the provinces like *les petits gens* in a Balzac story, in Paris you feel like Proust listening to morning sounds in the Faubourg St. Germain. If you live in a château you become a feudal lord, munificent and decorative; in a village inn you are a bourgeois sipping your *apéritif* on the sidewalk where the world goes by; in a Paris flat you are a romantic character out of Paul Bourget, with music by Fauré in the *salon;* in a left-bank hotel you always look out at trees like an old engraving, with the Beaux-Arts in the distance, or a church spire, a shaded garden or a corner café by Utrillo. In Paris you wander through streets that wander, you never feel that you are walking through blocks of duplicate buildings to arrive at another duplication. Houses don't seem to have been made by man, of bricks and mortar, but by nature, like trees.

Our lighthouse was no ivory tower—it had a more attractive isolation than that. We were in a balloon, in space, looking down at the life on earth as we floated by, but finding our own the most perfect kingdom. And for some reason I always thought of myself as the happiest person in the world.

2. Landscape and figures . . . but what events?

Just two that I would now call events. The first was that "strange great being." The second was a great idea.[*]

The first was a reality in terms of a fairy-tale. It gave my life an aspect of the unreal, for no one could believe

10

* There should be a third, really the first in terms of time: Jane Heap.

for a long time that such a perfect human bond was indeed a reality.

The second—the idea, the great theory—was a quest. It began as a search for an answer to a question. The answer we found became an experience that filled twenty years of our lives—an experience that has no ending and that can be described as "a life for a life."

Our question was this: "Can we ever know more about life than that it is 'a relationship between us and a mystery'?"

The answer was Yes.

We had sought an answer in the world's great books and had not found it. The Bible, we knew, contained all answers, but reading them had not set us on that "changed course of life" which was their object. The wisdom of the East, we knew, contained all the meanings, but we couldn't decipher them—the terminology put us off. We didn't understand that no one understands these texts until he has had his "event." Our event began when the great subject-matter was presented to us in a form that was right for our time, for our minds.

The nature of such an event lies in its slowness, and then, as you begin to understand what is happening to you, in its endlessness. It is the kind of event which, once sighted, can never be lost to sight. It goes along with you always, wherever you go, whatever you do, haunting you, goading you to deeper sight, however you may try to escape. There *is* no escape, because you know that no other reality can compare with it, can ever surpass it. This was the quest that was to become our life. Through all the years

11

it was to be our unavoidable preoccupation from day to day, from idea to idea, from experience to experience. It was to take us out of a dream and offer us, in its place, a new conception of life and death. And, finally, it was to change us from one kind of people into another kind.

"But you can't write *that* story," everyone said.

"Why not?" I said.

"Too intangible, too difficult, too outside ordinary experience."

"If that's all, I'll write it," I said.

"You won't find a publisher," they said.

"The public will like it," I said.

"You won't have a public because you won't have a publisher."

"I don't care," I said, "I must write it anyway."

I knew that to tell of it would be like trying to convey the emotion of music to someone who cannot feel it; not because it is difficult to convey, but because it is impossible. Nevertheless I was determined to try.

Perhaps I could make it clear, I thought, if I didn't tell it chronologically—as taking place, which of course it did, through all other experience. It could be lifted out of its space-frame and recorded separately. This would be a sort of super-truth, since the experience of an idea is set apart, and above, in your memory; you always talk of it as if it had been your whole story.

Besides, it is true that everyone lives his life in three parts; he has three centers of interest to fill. I could tell

12

how I filled mine, during all those years in France—my radiant physical life, my rapturous emotional life, my rabid mental life . . . three dimensions. I could tell of the three planes as if I had lived them separately instead of simultaneously; and then I could tell of our immense and difficult experience, suggesting what a fourth dimension of life might be.

3. As I began to plan my book I kept remembering one September day at the lighthouse when we talked of suicide. We had walked back from the château, through the forest, after lunching on *foie gras*, partridge and old burgundy, and we were realizing that we hadn't enough coffee for tomorrow's breakfast, that winter was coming and we had no place to go. We had had years of this kind of worry; perhaps it would be a rest to stop worrying and consider dying. All afternoon we talked of death, wondering whether we could find the courage, the wits and the worth to go on living. But toward evening talk revived us, as it always did. We were more determined than ever to survive, now that we had a deathless motive. Our life had been dream and mind. Now we were trying to transcend the mind and transmute the dream.

Georgette sat in the firelight and sang *"L'Invitation au Voyage"* in a muted voice. I looked at the fire, at the whitewashed walls and dark ceiling beams, at the blue plates on the wall and the old dresser with very old plates standing in rows, with roosters or roses painted on them; some were cracked and looked better that way.

13

Monique put another beech log on the fire. "Don't move," she said, "I will make dinner and bring you some wine." She came and went through the room, she put the red and white peasant cloth on the table. Then she lighted the lamp and brought bread, meat, cheese and the wine bottle. Mists from the Seine rose slowly upward and enclosed the lighthouse. . . .

"O SAISONS, Ô CHÂTEAUX"

I see myself, relentlessly American, going to France twenty-five years ago. Or rather, I don't see myself at all—I see what I saw then: Le Havre on a spring morning, painted cafés on the waterfront with tables over the sidewalks, yachts in the *bassin* before the flowerstalls, the terrace of the Grand Hotel Tortoni (now bombed to dust), houses with walled gardens and privacy even for the poor, which seemed to me at once a proof that France was going to be nicer than America.

We were going from Havre to Paris by car rather than by train because, at the moment, we were rich. (Or thought we were). Three months before in New York, after a series of concerts in her Washington Square *salon*, Georgette had been endowed for art, for life. The story of this sudden fairy-tale and its sudden end, two months later, is one of those extravaganzas that can happen only to people like us. Other people would understand neither its beginning nor its end, and if we should tell them what happened they would say, "There must be two sides to that story." But there are some stories that have only one side. They are the stories no one believes. Georgette always said that people would believe anything provided it wasn't true.

With the art endowment we had been urged to buy the château that most pleased us in all France, use it as a *pied-à-terre* and spend our winters in America where Georgette would give concerts and lectures. When the endowment was withdrawn she fell ill, as one always does when endowments are withdrawn—because of the reasons for which they are always withdrawn. So now we were to have no home—château or *chaumière;* no exquisite concerts or flaming lecture tours. The only thing left was to take refuge for the moment in a family château. This would have consternated Georgette if it hadn't been for my enthusiasm. I had always felt that the type of physical life for which I am best fitted was to be found, made to order, in a French château. Besides, I was tired of New York; I was tired of the *Little Review* which, with *Ulysses,* had reached the highwater mark for our generation; I wanted a period of calm and quiet, time to look over my life and see what it was about.

On this spring morning we took the upper road out of Le Havre, instead of the one along the river, and drove through the farm and château country of Normandy. The roads were white, the fields pale yellow and filled with small red poppies. I can still smell the dust and straw from the open arched gates of farm courtyards, I can still hear the crunch of heavy two-wheeled carts pulled by fat white horses, one behind the other, and the hard voices of peasants calling out to them. Sometimes white geese strolled across the road and we had to stop to let them pass; sometimes we paused before a long avenue of birch trees leading to an old *manoir* standing in fields and orchards, or a village church surrounded by its graveyard, facing a brown café with white beams and red geraniums in the windows and a sign across the front—*"Ici on boit et on mange."* We came into St. Romains de Colbus and saw an inn called "L'Hôtel de la Bonne Societé." Ten kilometres farther on we circled down through a park-like country of great trees to our destination—the fortress-château of Tancarville.

This first château in which I was to live at intervals for the next twenty years was on the Seine. It was built in the eleventh century, was used by William the Conqueror as a fortress, by Richard the Lion-Hearted as a refuge, and by Charles IX as a residence for Agnès Sorel who gave birth to his child in the Tour des Aigles. Mary Stuart is supposed to have been imprisoned in the same tower, and Elizabeth of England lived for a summer in the Tour Carré[*] —embroideries she made there can still be seen in a museum in Rouen.

We drove through the entrance gates set within round towers where prisoners died slowly a long time ago. The stone walls were covered with roses, and above on higher ground I saw turrets, towers, arcades and buttresses, ruins of early Norman castle life against a white cloud. I ran to explore the ruins and found beautiful fireplaces suspended in air, filled with grasses and flowers instead of flames; stone window-seats in tiers of floorless rooms and spiral stairways leading to the sky. Later I approached the

[*] Probably not true, but the family in the chateau swore that it was.

17

château slowly, as in my Indiana childhood I had opened
a book of Howard Pyle's painted palaces. The *salon* windows were twenty feet high; looking through them into the
center of the room I saw a round table covered with silk
to the floor; on it—shining with so faint a light that the
ceiling was invisible—stood a small kerosene lamp. This
was my introduction to French economy.

The bedrooms were all on the Seine and each one had
a dressing-room on the corridor and an antichambre from
which, as you entered, you could contemplate your canopied bed. Mine was Empire, draped in grey and yellow
silk, closing me in to a view of white fireplace, a long blue
sky, a dark river with a red light and a green one on the
sandbar at the curve. Lace covered the marble of the
mantle, hanging down to the height of invisible flames.
Candles glittered in a tall mirror and on the bed-table stood
another kerosene lamp with a pink shade. That night I
lighted it and lay in bed and looked and listened, breathed
or held my breath, in peace. I shall always remember that
first night in my favorite château. There was space in it,
though not the space I experienced later at the lighthouse.
To me a château is in the world, a lighthouse is in the universe. From château windows the days look high and the
nights deep, but at the lighthouse the days looked wide and
the nights high.

I don't know, exactly, what Rimbaud meant by "O
saisons, ô châteaux." I only know that for me the sun and
moon are different on a château terrace, the seasons more
formal, space and peace reveal their interdependence. A
château may stand alone in the country but you never feel

you are in the country when you stay there; you feel you
are in *a* country—a château is a world apart. The life
lived in such a place has no purpose, but it has form; the
hours pass and you like to watch them go by. But at the
lighthouse it was the seasons I liked to watch; there I had
no feeling of being in a world but the sensation of living
on a planet. Climate and hours are worldly divisions to me,
seasons and days are above them. You always know what
time it is in a château because of the boredom that threat-
ens every hour of château life. It was a boredom I came
to love.

At first I found it redundant to meet house guests in
corridors, they always stopped me to say "The sun shines,
it is gay." If it were raining they said, "It rains, it is sad."
I wanted to answer "I see that the sun shines, I see that the
rain falls, so let us discuss whether sun is always gay and
rain always sad." Later I came to like these constatations,
they had their place, indispensable to the permanent charm
of the environment like the engravings of the *Muses* and
Helen of Troy and *Richelieu* and *Leda* and *La Sortie
du Bain* that had hung on the walls for forty years, the
Richelieu always a little crooked; one of the first things
I did every year was to straighten it. I began to look forward to the repeated gestures and exclamations as I did to
the recurrence of seasons, the succession of well-served
meals and badly-played chess games, the nights spent in
canopied beds and the days spent in family quarrels. I became a connoisseur of family quarrels in château salons.

The quarrels were always as petty as the salons were
grandiose. The weather was usually the subject of con-

tention—yesterday was not so hot as today, it had or had not rained two days ago. The châtelaine (Georgette's sister) and her husband often ended an evening in such a fury over the barometer that they avoided saying good-night to each other. They had only this to do, it was something, all their lives they had done nothing. Born in châteaux where nothing ever happened, they had moved from one to another with the seasons, the weather the only event in all of them.

The châtelaine had been exposed to certain real events in her early life but she hadn't noticed them. When she divorced her first husband he stipulated that she leave behind her three children and never see them again. She kept her word without difficulty. Twenty years later, in a Rouen pastry-shop with her cousin, she was choosing cakes beside three young women. When they left the shop her cousin whispered, "Those are your daughters." "Really?" she said, and didn't go to the door to see what they looked like. On the other hand she was criminally interested in other people's events, especially letters. She opened her son's letters whenever they looked personally important. She didn't steam them open and reseal them but read them and threw them away.

Her husband was too phlegmatic either to take part in, or prevent, these acts. He was fifty when I first saw him, strong and fond of his wine, never ill a day in fifty years, never inclined to do anything with twenty-four hours but eat, drink and not be merry. His fortune was inherited, there was no work in the world he could understand or do, and he never came downstairs until lunchtime. I once asked him what he did all morning. "I don't know," he said, "I get dressed." He hadn't taken a bath because the bath (one bathroom to twenty bedrooms) didn't work either. His valet handed him his clothes, everything was handed to him, I never saw him put out his arm in a spontaneous gesture toward any object. He sat only in the deepest armchairs and, once installed, he didn't reach for the newspaper on the table beside him, it was handed to him. If there was no servant about, his wife handed it, or one of the vague young girls always to be found in a château in the suspicious rôle of *gouvernante*. He had had only one mental interest through the years—science. He owned two small scientific treatises which he had read over and over. One was entitled *Perpetual Motion*. All the passages relating to energy had been forcefully underscored in red ink.

There was another family member, also a millionaire with châteaux of his own but with a preference for this one in Tancarville. He was much respected in the family because he was nervous, had indigestion and insomnia, had hysteria if he ever found himself in a draft, and because he wrote books. He wore a plaid shawl, like Mallarmé, counted his *haricots verts* and never ate more than eight. He always spent the month of October in this château on the Seine; otherwise he couldn't turn out his annual book. He would write a few lines in his room before lunch— never more than half a page. After lunch he would try to sleep for half an hour, and not succeed; then he took a measured walk, never more than half a mile, *aller et retour*. After tea he sat in his room before a fire, never more than half awake; he enjoyed the twilight and planned what he would write next day. In the salon before dinner he would stand in front of the fire, musing over his perfect day, his shawl discarded, declaiming Racine in a voice of confident emotion: "I alone, I say, and it is enough." I always joined him in speculation about the pleasantest moment of the day. "Coffee after lunch," I would say, "just before the chess game." "No, no," he said, "the *apéritif* before lunch, as we wait for the second bell." But he never took the *apéritif*.

In winter the most hilarious moment of the day for me was ten o'clock at night. Everyone would decide that sleep was imperative. But to reach the bedrooms they had to leave the salon fire and pass through cold corridors. Preparations were made for the journey, heavy coats put on and mufflers tied about throats. Then a servant brought hats. The man who made no gestures waited by the fire, his arms hanging. His wife would choose a hat for him, any hat, one of her own, and drop it on his head. Then, and then only, the salon doors were opened, the procession went out single-file, the climb upward began. I, coatless and hatless and an object of alarm, led the ascent, running ahead up the stairs from where I could look down and watch them trudging upward, candles held like torches, as if through the snow and ice of an Alpine night.

Georgette had spent too many summers in French châteaux, she would have preferred a studio in Washington Square without enough to eat. But since there was no prospect of giving concerts anywhere except in the privacy of

the home, we accepted the Tower of the Eagles as home
and concert-hall. After the protoplasmic life of the day we
took refuge in this tower named for eagles and determined
to soar there. We soared at night; we came to life at midnight, less like eagles perhaps than like the mice in animated cartoons. We let ourselves go to music. We opened
the windows and Georgette sang toward the ilex tree, the
Schubert Serenade rose high over the ruins.

If we were exultant mice by night we were discreet
ones by day. There was no other way for an American to
meet the avalanche of French nature—human nature—
which descended upon me. (Georgette didn't count as
French, she considered them an alien race.) If I had tried
to exist among these French bourgeois as anything approaching what up to now I had regarded as the human
species, I wouldn't have survived beyond the first encounter. I found it necessary to imagine that I was in an
asylum and accept the life there as uninfluencable.

Every situation in this demented world had a com-
plication, these people would have had no pleasures otherwise. When we drove through the country they brought the
car to a full stop to ask directions of passers-by, going into
questions and answers as if they had the day for it, as if
it were a game to begin over as soon as one side had won.
What confused me was that neither side ever won, they
never managed to understand each other's French. When
we drove on we turned to the right when we had been told
to turn left, though *droite* and *gauche* sounded nothing
alike to me. Some cried left, some cried right, others had
already forgotten what had been said, but all joined in the

dispute with strong personal abuse. Half a mile farther on they repeated the same questionnaire, then we would stop for tea in order to debate all issues of confusion. "He no longer hears," a wife would say in her husband's hearing, "what a thing it is to become senile." "You say what?" cried the husband who had heard everything but had no repartee. They moved like bodies under water from the car to the tea-table, and the next long slow scene developed over the waiter's tip. Being in a bad humor because they were lost, no one wanted to tip; or if someone had drunk only half a cup of tea he wanted the other half subtracted from the bill. Hands under the sea fumbled toward unattainable pockets, heads turned in slow reproach toward the unmoving *garçon*, bodies waved toward each other in silent protest as they dragged out their smallest change and slow-motioned their way back to the car. I always left a normal tip which they never noticed, they were too absorbed in choosing invectives against the *patron*, the *garçon*, the place—reverting to the left and right debate as responsible for tea that cost fifty centimes more than it would have cost in that place which was either to the right or the left, "alas, we will never know, when you promenade with a man who has become gaga you risk a great deal."

Our châtelaine was a resourceful woman, with a talent for turning facts into fancies. Even without this gift it was complex to deal with her, you had to remember always to say the opposite of what you wanted, or wanted her to want, in order to bring about what everyone more or less wanted. This was often possible, but it was impossible to extricate yourself from the meshes of her masterful lying.

Sometimes she involved you in a confusion over natural laws, like the angora cat episode. I had had a black angora kitten that died. The concierge had a scrawny black cat with such brutally blunted fur that I commented on its ugliness. "You didn't think it was ugly last year," said the liar. "Last year!" I said, "I never saw it before." "Never saw it before! It's your cat!" "My cat!" I said, "my cat died." "Oh, no, it didn't, the concierge took it, this is it." "But my cat was angora, with beautiful long soft hair." "Yes, of course, this one is angora, only it has rubbed its hair off against the tree trunks." I looked around at the others, expecting them to support me. No one said anything. It had been years since she had been contradicted.

What mystified me was her object, though that was obvious enough in the affair of the phonograph record. Someone had sent me "Rain" from America. It made a great hit with the family, so much so that it disappeared from my record case into theirs. I inquired into this and the châtelaine said I must have lost it—"You can see for yourself I have only mine here, it is marked with a cross as I mark all my *disques*." She showed me a big white cross in the center of my record. In France you are not supposed to say, "But you never heard of that record until I played it for you, I'll just take it back." I said instead, "You're sure this is your record?" "Oh, yes," she said, "I bought it long before you came." "That's curious," I said, "it isn't out yet in France. And you see this is an American *disque*, the title and words are in English." "Of course, I forgot, someone sent it to me from America." She said

25

this without wavering, looking me strongly in the eye. I looked at the others as usual, out of habit, without hope. The husband looked away, some looked sad, others made silent appeals to American chivalry. Georgette took me aside and said, "You'll never get it back without stealing it." I got the key to the billiard-room closet from the butler and late that night I broke in and took my record, feeling like a thief.

During my first month in this château I began to be haunted by the absence of a certain human quality I had always found in America—the impulse of generosity. Having just come from a nation where everyone is generous in one form or another, having kept the *Little Review* alive for years through the benevolence of hundreds of people in Chicago, San Francisco and New York, I was accustomed to a race that would rather give than not give. But I noticed that these French people never made a generous gesture toward anyone, not even toward themselves. At first I tried to disregard this, thinking they might all be living under some strain unknown to me; then I began to count the opportunities they found to be ungenerous; after that I could see nothing but their faces going empty as they sidestepped opportunity. If they agreed about nothing else on earth they were all in harmony about allowing no franc to escape from the family circle. Servants who had worn themselves out for forty years in the family service were sent away to seek charity when they became too old or ill to work. One, at seventy-five, went to live with her sister in one room, and since there was only one bed she slept on two chairs. There were at least a dozen empty servant beds in the château, but no one would have dreamed of sending her one; there was the question of cartage, and then they might never get the bed back. I spoke of the kindness of English and American families, of the pension they would have considered a duty and a pleasure to settle upon the faithful servant. This was received badly. "They are too good, those people, nothing obliges them to do such a thing." "Oblige" is a highly-respected verb in the French language; it means: no obligation exists except that imposed by law. I know a French lawyer who illustrates the attitude. He asked Georgette one day how she was managing to live, knowing that she had just emerged from pneumonia and had no money even for food. She explained that her life had been saved by Monique's pleadings which had finally extracted a monthly sum from her brother. The lawyer asked how much. She told him. "Very little," he commented, "but after all it is kind; nothing obliges him to do it." "That is true," Georgette said, "nothing does— nothing but sentiment, the fact of wealth as against poverty, the preservation of a fellow creature—in this case his nearest and dearest blood relation." "Yes, naturally, but all the same the law doesn't oblige him to do it."

Of course these people with whom I was living couldn't be blamed directly. Avarice had been preached to them and practised before them for generations. But of all their economic codes I found their ideas of sex economy the most startling. One branch of the family had three sons and three châteaux, but the father engaged one mistress for the three sons—and included himself in the bargain. They were all amused at my shocked reaction. "What would you?" they said. "Nothing extraordinary," I said. "I would have liked a mistress for each son, with whom he was at least mildly in love, and as many for the father as he felt necessary." "Oh," they laughed, *"ce n'est pas la peine."* (It isn't worth all that.)

For eight months of the year the Normandy château stood empty, though open and supervised by concierges and gardeners. I asked the family why they didn't urge friends to live in it during the winter and spring—there was one couple among their childhood friends to whom it would have been a godsend. "Ah, no," they said, "that uses electricty." (This was later, when they had electric light.) "But aren't you willing to pay for that small amount of electricity?" I insisted. "Ah no," they said, "the electricity already costs enough when we are here, we're not going to pay for it when we're not here." "But I'm sure your friends will be glad to pay for it—much easier for them than to pay rent in Paris." "No," they said, "we feel better when no one is here." If I persisted until they felt they should feel shame, they said that their friends had been asked to live in the château and had ungratefully refused, that they hated châteaux, that they were thieves, or communists, or had firebug tendencies. When they were publicly accused of allowing Georgette to live in extreme poverty they announced that they supported her in extreme luxury. When incredulity was expressed at this statement they explained that she squandered her money on cocktails (for which she had a well-known Gallic loathing).

I managed to surmount these experiences, even to extract a certain diversion from their freshness, but there was one that made me cry. It was about gardens. Georgette always had an organic relation to gardens, they revived her. Since she had long ago had to part with abbeys and *manoirs* and beautiful Provençal houses she had been without gardens, but she always thought of them. Her brother had a Peter Ibbetson garden in Passy and a house of fifteen rooms in which he too "felt better" when no one was there. One spring afternoon he and Georgette were reviving themselves among his trees and flowers. "Well," he said, "you'll have a garden one day, *ma chère*—in the cemetery, ha, ha, ha."

During my first summer of château life in Normandy I saw just one gesture of liberality. One night at dinner the fish was superior but for some reason limited; it was remarked that Georgette had almost none. The butler went to the kitchen for more, reported that there was no more, and the situation was about to be dismissed as insoluble when the man of many gardens had an inspiration. "Wait," he said, eyeing his large portion, "you must have some of mine." He put part of his fish on Georgette's plate. As she thanked him I saw her face stiffen. I looked at her plate.

"But it's the head," I said, before I could stop myself.

By this time I was as repelled by the French as I was attracted by their country. I began to make a collection of economy stories, chiefly of old Rouenaise families, all of them rich. One was about some people who lived for years in the darkest house in Rouen. Their friends got tired of visiting them in the gloom and begged them to move to a new house. They couldn't, they explained, because their present house had a great virtue—it stood on a corner where there was a strong street lamp. When they went upstairs at night this lamp lighted the bedrooms and they could undress by its rays instead of lighting the candles. Thus for years they saved a daily half-hour of candlelight.

Later on even the peasants in Normandy had electricity, but they went to bed at dark rather than turn it on. Many of them were rich; I even heard of some who were known to have hidden as much as a hundred thousand francs in their houses—they didn't trust banks. And there was the story of the mayor of a small village who had saved and hidden two million francs. He placed the money, in hundred franc notes, between the pages of notebooks and glued the pages together; no one, not even his wife, knew where he hid the notebooks. His last gesture after a meal was to amass all the crumbs on the table into a cup, and his first gesture at the next meal was to eat those crumbs before he allowed himself a new piece of bread.

In a château not far from ours there was a very rich man who had been dying all summer. He knew he was dying, his wife knew it and talked to him as if he were already dead. She kept reminding him that he would never drink again; but this didn't make the desired impression —he still kept the keys to the wine-cellar locked in his bedroom, allowing his family of six only one bottle every two days. When they had guests they didn't ask for the keys, knowing that he wouldn't offer an extra bottle since he couldn't drink with them. Everyone was embarrassed by this situation, but no one cared to think how simple it would be to order wine from the village. When the hunting-season opened his wife asked him if she couldn't give away five of his ten pairs of boots to the *garde-chasse,* or the gardener, or even to his friends who were out shooting for him in inferior boots. Every day she would say, "But why not, since you won't wear them again?" And every day he answered, "Never."

In my next château—in Neuilly-sur-Seine—I entered another fairytale. As I opened the grilled gate and stepped into the courtyard I felt like a child who has gone a long way through a dark forest and in its depth comes upon a palace waiting in the enchanted gloom. Approaching slowly, I opened great doors and stood within a glass dome, round and vast, and then there was light. It came from all sides and from many levels, it came from crystal and glass and silver candelabra, from chandeliers of Venetian glass with a hundred bulbs that rocketed showers of light; it came from mirrors that cascaded light like fountains.

This château was called Le Palais des Muses—or Le Pavillon des Muses—and Louis XIV is supposed to have stayed in it. Later it belonged to Robert de Montesquieu who gave fêtes in its *salons* which are still remembered in Paris. The "family" had had it directly from Montesquieu and it, if not they, retained the splendor of old days. We discovered an apartment in a wing which, I believe, no one had ever taken the trouble to explore. With our usual zest we made it into a perfect home. It would be our *pied-à-terre* in France—an oasis in which we could always revive after a too-dry season in the desert of the practical world.

Fortified by this assurance from the family, we went back to New York in October and Georgette set out to fulfill concert engagements scheduled before the evaporation of her art endowment. They were now to take place with no guarantee except expenses, and they did take place—with super gallantry, super worry, super effort and super art. I remember these beautiful concerts in cities and towns all the way from New York to San Francisco; I remember critics writing that Georgette Leblanc, if asked to, could sing the multiplication table as exquisitely as Pallisy handled porcelain. I remember trains flying, Negro porters convulsed with joy over the French language. I remember reporters assigned to interview a French woman about love and Georgette happily resigned to informing them. I remember hotel rooms furnished in roses, and a Beverly Hills bungalow among orange trees, where our French maid ate every item on the menu for a month and had to buy a large dress to wear back to Paris. I remember Claire Eames disguised as Queen Elizabeth; Douglas Fairbanks, Sr., on the United Artists' lot, leaping fences as if he were walking over them; Charlie Chaplin giving dinners and charades and playing "Armand" to Georgette's "Camille." I remember deserts more brilliant than painting and forests larger than life. I remember an inconceivable Grand Canyon. I remember talking with every kind of human being produced on the American continent.

32

And then, because there was no more money for concerts—but chiefly because our great event had now begun—we went back to France.

But in Neuilly the family invited us not to stay: they were leaving for the Riviera where they had rented another château and they would feel better if the Muses remained closed. So our apartment and thirty other rooms stood empty for six months, their beauty visible only to an evil-smelling concierge whose duties were heavily increased by having to open and close fifty windows a day to air a house in which no one lived. The house in the Passy garden was also to be closed, with its fifteen empty rooms, and I began to feel like a communist. We went back to our little left-bank hotel; it was without sun, but in imagination we lived in a lavish movement from one to another of those forty-five magnificent empty rooms whose every window opened upon sun and trees.

Georgette received an offer from an unknown manager for a concert tour of Italy. We left for Genoa where the first concert took place in an enormous opera house to which no one had been invited, as the manager had refrained from advertising. This shocked us, but he promised that all would be different in Turin where he had carefully arranged everything. He had, even to the careful stealing of Georgette's mink coat. Thereupon he left Turin; the hotel manager went into hiding; the police arrived two hours after being called and confined their search to our trunks, on the theory that we had stolen the coat ourselves.

A hotel clerk said they once had a guest who complained that his hat had been stolen; everyone was searching for it when the guest discovered he was holding it in his hands. We held out our hands to prove they held no mink coat, but this appeared to prove only that we had never had one. Georgette explained that her coat was her only house, she never left it for fear of taking cold. D'Annunzio and Mussolini were called upon to help, but the investigation came to nothing and we left for Paris—Georgette in borrowed furs—where the papers announced that the stolen coat had been invented for publicity. We felt we had touched bottom.

I remember that New Year's Eve. We had only a few francs left, a little worn courage, and no plans. We were too sad to see anyone, we decided to go to a quiet café on the Luxembourg Gardens and review our possibilities. We ordered *café liègeois* and made plans which, this time, ought to succeed. But soon I noticed that Monique had tears in her eyes. Then I noticed Georgette looking at me with a long look, and tears came into her eyes. Then I felt that I must cry too, so I did. We all cried for a little while, then we felt better and went home.

In desperation I decided to conceive and execute an appeal which might move even a French family to action. I wrote to the man of many gardens, paraphrasing a poet to help me: "There is always something to do instead of writing letters that rob her of sleep. Think, with Monique and me, of Rilke's prayer in 'The Death of the Poet':

'Present her with a tender, a confident day,
Lead her close to a garden,
Compensate her too-heavy nights,
Preserve her.' "

His response to this was a three-hour talk with Georgette, beginning with a reference to my insolent letter. Then he talked of many topics, including the weather. Then he drew from an inside coat pocket a five hundred franc note, saying that perhaps she could use it. He talked for another hour, chiefly about his trip to Italy, how comfortable his new car had been (a new one yearly); how comfortable the trains had been (he always travelled halfway by train, his chauffeur following in the car, since long distances by motor were fatiguing). After the second hour he drew out five notes of one hundred francs each, from an outside pocket, as if he had forgotten having them. When she rose to go he fumbled a long time in an inside pocket and drew out two one hundred franc notes, saying she had better take them too. As she reached the door he fumbled again and called her back to offer three more one hundred franc notes, from another pocket, making fifteen hundred in all. The decision to give the complete sum had taken several hours, but the distribution of it in several pockets proved that the good deed had been premeditated.

With the fifteen hundred francs we found a small apartment and achieved comforts. I remember this epoch as one of the most satisfyingly unreal of my existence. As it happened, I knew no Americans in Paris; I had no clothes, I had no necessity to leave the apartment and I spent the days at the piano arranging new concert programs. Every day I dressed in the same costume—dark blue workman's jeans on which I wore a yellow flower.

Once I was amazed to find I hadn't left the apartment for two weeks, even to walk around the block—life in the interior was too absorbing, a day was like an hour, the piano effaced time. After a day's work there was the evening in the little salon that always smelled of eucalyptus leaves, the coffee on the Empire *guéridon*, the lampshade of blue flowers, the books to read while taxis honked in the street below, the talk of music and the plans for next day's work on concerts that were never to be given. I have heard adults tell children that life can never be what they wish or hope. I should like to correct this malefic and irresponsible statement. For eight months I lived this life of my childhood's imagination and the only words I can find today to describe it are these: the final revised edition of perfect happiness.

Sometimes at dusk I put on an old suit, too shabby to expose to the light of day, and walked through the streets of the Left Bank, along the quais, past lighted antique shops; sometimes I bought a bag of roasted chestnuts and sat on a café terrace to drink not only beer but the sights and sounds and smells of the city I loved—the city of love, loveliness, liberty and light. Everyone loves Venice, everyone loves to be in Budapest, but Paris is the city in which one loves to live. Sometimes I think this is because it is the only city in the world where you can step out of a railway station—the Gare D'Orsay—and see, simultaneously, the chief enchantments: the Seine with its bridges and bookstalls, the Louvre, Nôtre Dame, the Tuileries Gardens, the Place de la Concorde, the beginning of the Champs Elysées—nearly everything except the Luxembourg Gardens and the Palais Royal. But what other city offers as much as you leave a train? and where, by merely raising your eyes, can you see in a city's center a sky as pure as a pastoral?

Among all other reasons there is one, to me, that explains Paris as a place of personal freedom. Other cities (except London) have their cafés, but the cafés of Paris provide for the life of the mind. They are institutions to man's necessity to "leave home," not once but daily. On every street corner you find this refuge from domesticity, at the end of the day even the most unassertive bourgeois can free himself from family life, imagining that all is not yet lost. And when you can spend your troubled midnight on a red plush *banquette,* drinking your coffee in a tall glass, watching the impersonal waiters with tired intelligent faces, long accustomed to the mind's renewal under the too-bright lights . . . this is a city for those romantic reflexes in which it would be pleasant to live forever, and even to die.

I was never an expatriate—the word had no meaning to me. I felt that I had been born in Paris and that I could never, willingly or wonderfully, live anywhere else.

2. We couldn't keep the flat. In the spring we went north to the château on the Seine, where the family was moving from one financial crisis to another. One night after dinner I went back to the salon for a book and nearly stumbled over the châtelaine and her husband who were sitting in complete darkness—"to save electricity."

The next day we turned our backs on the château and took a walk along the Seine. Half a mile away we went into an inn and sat down on the terrace to brood upon avarice. Then I looked up at the sky. High above us, on a *falaise*, pinned upon a cloud, I saw a glass dome. It had a small round cupola on top, like Russian churches. "What's that?" I asked the *patron*. "It's an old lighthouse," he said. "Empty?" I asked quickly. "Oh yes, a man and his wife used to live there, but that was years ago. It's too isolated, no one wants to live there now."

"Only we," Georgette and I said simultaneously. We began to run toward the clouds. The only way up was a short steep road which ended at a peasant inn. The peasants were Norman, which means that all projects are impossible—lighthouses in the sky more than others. "You can't even get up the path, the brambles have grown too high," they said. I asked for a scythe and cut our way up easily. The peasants didn't follow, they felt danger on all sides—so the lighthouse emerged for us privately from brambles, high grass and trees. We looked first at it and then at what was around it, which appeared to be a new heaven and a new earth.

We walked back to the château hand in hand, in recognition of manna still falling, in solidarity against obstacles which might arise. For us there was no flaw in the lighthouse: inside it looked like a sympathetic rabbit hutch, outside like a chapel in the sunlight. Windows and doors and whitewash were all it needed, and all we needed was the money to buy it. The owner wouldn't sell, but he would rent, and we had a long discussion about terms. The last tenant had paid eighty francs a year; we would have to pay fifty francs a month.

The family promised to help with the repairs, alarmed, I believe, by my aggressions. They half kept their promise and we half moved in—with doors and windows but nothing else. We spent the summer arranging the "nothing" into paradise.

Then winter came. The family had bought a new château in Saint-Germain—a large and beautiful Empire house where Napoleon once lived. It stood among forest trees, had thirty-five rooms and a suspended terrace garden—a hidden garden at the top of the house set within lilac bushes as tall as trees. This garden was reached through a living-room solarium with the light and air (from windows on four sides) that doctors had prescribed for Georgette. At this epoch we were more determined than ever to sustain life and I remember the bargain that was arranged. "I will pay no rent," I was surprised to hear Georgette say with new strength, "I will pay for food, service, electricity, gas, telephone, but I consider that the family should consider it a privilege to offer me this unused space." There was a silence that implied acceptance and we went to live in the tree sanatorium. I played innumerable games of chess as my passport to welcome, but since I had more enthusiasm for chess than anyone else this only increased the charm of life for me.

That charm in retrospect is composed of lilacs and

nightingales. I suppose there are never more than two nightingale memories in any life, there is the first one and the last one. It was my last personal nightingale that sang here. It sang from midnight until dawn and I slept only before midnight and after dawn, trying to find other words besides "blithe spirit."

In March the trees turned from black to a mist of Corot green, in April lilacs drenched the gardens, in May wistaria flowers blew into the windows and we would have felt in paradise (again) if it hadn't been for the depression that developed about baths. We paid six francs for every bath (hotel price), but a contention arose about the number we took. We cut our necessities to three a week but this was also criticized. We reduced to two a week but even this didn't lighten the atmosphere. Our bathroom had a heater which was lighted by a servant at six in the morning in order to produce hot water by nine o'clock. One morning at seven I was awakened by stealthy movements near the bathroom. I went to investigate and found the châtelaine poking her head under our heater to see if the gas was burning. She wasn't embarrassed but explained she was sure we took more baths than we declared and she meant to exercise a rigid bath-control. She laughed at my stern face and explained that she was very clever in looking out for her own interests. While I was trying to understand her pride in this superfluous self-description she moved away, still laughing cleverly, "Ah ha, we shall see, we shall see." Her anger was great, but her enjoyment of her *métier* (economy) even greater.

I had long ceased to answer these jibes as they deserved, because of results more tragic than the jibes. So I laughed too and said I would use cold water in the future and hoped this would in some way make everyone happier.

One night I had a guest for dinner whose happiness depended on brandy after coffee. Since this guest always brought gifts for my hosts I felt that I might send to the kitchen for a small glass of brandy without upsetting our fragile *entente cordiale*. The cook came up in distress. "It's just that monsieur's present bottle of brandy is almost empty; if I take any out of it he will notice, and if I open a new bottle and take any out he will notice that too." "Well," I said, "there's a way out of this impasse, we'll play a joke on monsieur. Here are five francs. Take them to him and say that I want to buy five francs' worth of brandy for my guest." We waited for her to come back with the brandy, perhaps two brandies, a message about what a pleasure it was to offer it, and of course the five francs. After a long interval she came back with one very small glass of brandy, no message and no money. "And the five francs?" I asked. She began to laugh uncontrollably. "Monsieur took them, then he measured out the brandy in the smallest glass." "He didn't say anything?" "Not a word, he just put out his hand for the money."

After four months of this life we became melancholy. It was impossible to work, someone was always knocking at our doors to see if we were burning electricity too early in the evening, or if a servant had sneaked us some of the family firewood. It was impossible to concentrate on

41

chess in the evenings because the servants would be summoned to the salon for an inquest over the fourteen chocolates that had been left in the box, who had taken two of them? One of the oldest servants was always coming to tell us how her account books had been tampered with, to make it appear that her wages had been paid when they hadn't been. She wept, we interceded, always without result—except the strain on our nervous systems.

In May the tension broke. One evening someone telephoned me from Paris. The next morning I was interrupted by a knock and the announcement that I hadn't inscribed a telephone call to Paris. "But I didn't call Paris," I said, "Paris called me." "But we happened to hear that you were cut off and then you called back." "On the contrary," I said, "when I was cut off I waited until Paris called me back." "But R. says he heard you call Paris." R. was the man who never heard anything. It now appeared that, crouched behind closed double doors, he had heard words I never said.

I expressed my opinion—partly, I suppose, because it was May. Though May was a cold month in Normandy I knew we could keep warm in the lighthouse and I knew that my honest words would result in hinted hopes that we leave. But before we left, the châtelaine reverted to the telephone drama. She said she had been informed of new official rulings, that all telephone calls now had to be paid for twice—once by the person calling and again by the person called. By a ruse I got her into a postoffice and asked an official, in her hearing, about the new law. He looked as disconcerted as if I had been insane, but my hostess maintained her poise and said that if the new ruling wasn't yet in effect it would be soon, a higher authority had told her so.

3. Somehow, somewhere, during these last two years we had each managed to finish a book— Georgette's *Souvenirs* * and my *Thirty Years' War*. Our royalties now made possible another château venture— this time one of our own. Or so we thought.

One day during a promenade in the forest of Saint-Germain the family had discovered a château-pavillion which Louis XV had used as a hunting-lodge. They promptly rented it, not to live in but simply because it was beautiful and they felt better in feeling that they owned it. This family, at moments, was patterned after my own heart; there were points in which it perfectly paralleled my personal ancestry—my mother too always felt better when she rented all available beautiful houses.

I remember the day we first went to see this little château. It stood quite alone in the forest and its classic beauty was touching. Georgette walked all around it, looking at its perfect proportions with tears in her eyes. It had been built for François Premier and was later used by Louis XV and Louis XVI. Madame de Pompadour's letters contain descriptions of the "three superb *salons*" and "the immense and beautiful *sousterrains*," built like a cathedral. "*Le reste,*" she added, "*est peu de chose.*"

---

* *Souvenirs: My Life with Maeterlinck.* Georgette Leblanc. E. P. Dutton & Co., New York, 1931.

The rest, for me, was adorable—alcoved bedrooms, handsome fireplaces, a top floor with Jean Jacques Rousseau windows, all looking into a forest of chestnut trees. Four wide avenues penetrated the woods at right angles to the four sides of the pavillion; in the one before the *rotonde* Louis XV stood and called to his favorite deer and as it appeared shot it through the heart to prove his prowess. La Pompadour wrote of driving out in state from Paris— it took them three hours to do the twenty kilometres; then they spent the evenings gambling in the small *salon.* At a later epoch Marie Antoinette was presented to Louis XVI in the beautiful *rotonde* and a *fête de fiançailles* given. Later Voltaire came often to the Muette, and still later Madame de Staël brought Benjamin Constant out to talk (or to listen) in all the rooms.

Besides being called the Muette, this château had another name—La Folie d'Artois. Louis XV gave it finally to the dukes of Artois, and a *"folie"* in the old sense meant a *pavillon* or *manoir* sympathetic for hunting, or other, rendez-vous. For us it was a *folie* in a still later sense of the word.

The family offered to rent it to us at half price. Of course as soon as we moved in we were invited to pay full price and we lived from folly to folly. La Muette was ranked as a *monument historique,* which means that you can't repaint the woodwork yourself, no matter how impeccable your taste or your technique; you must wait for the Beaux Arts to paint it for you. One of the principal talents of the Beaux Arts is to make you wait. After we moved in we waited a year and a half for them, and then

44

we waited for them to return and finish what they hadn't done—though we had to move out before this culmination.

At the end of September, 1930, we were installed in this lovely uninhabitable château. We gathered furniture, curtains and chandeliers from the storehouse attics of other châteaux; we had a well in the forest, we had candles, and we had firewood on all sides. The Beaux Arts promised to send their workmen in October; by Christmas everything would be restored, repaired, cleaned, painted, papered.

All through October we waited for the workmen. No workmen appeared, no telephone calls with the Beaux Arts could establish any relation between that institution, us, the Muette and workmen. Finally the Beaux Arts promised to begin work in December. December passed, no workmen came. We spent our time seeing cabinet ministers. This would have been all right except that in France no matter what minister you see it is always the wrong one. Each minister was impressed, polite, reassuring—everything would be done, someone else would do it, and it would be done promptly. January passed, I don't know why we didn't freeze to death with the wind howling through the holes, but we had no other place to live and we had paid rent to live in this one—rent in advance being our idea of promptness. In February we learned that we had been kept waiting for what is known as the *devis*— the itemized estimate of what is to be done. Each minister had known this—it is the custom of the country—but none had cared to mention it, preferring to let us believe that the workmen would arrive in hordes at seven o'clock on Monday morning. We were told this so often that we always got up early on Monday to welcome the prompt hordes that were to live in our attic while the work went on instead of going home at night, thus increasing their efficiency.

In March we were told that the Beaux Arts had never intended to send their workmen during the short days of winter. In April, with longer light, they would arrive, work, and finish.

In May we went to see more ministers. Throughout June we continued. In July no more ministers could be seen because they had all left Paris. In October we received official papers that the *devis* was now complete and work would begin before Christmas. In March two workmen arrived and it was they, symbol of hordes, who accomplished the restoration of the Muette. It took them many months and they took the months calmly, never sleeping in the attic, spending not only the nights but much of the day with their families or with each other in the forest, drinking cider under the flowering chestnut trees.

During these ages of time we passed through many dramas with the four elements, but the water drama was the most national. The bathroom had been installed by former tenants in a small second-floor salon; it had charm but nothing in it functioned except a large hot-water boiler which, when heated from the kitchen below, thundered with such force that the plumber told us not to go near it unless we wanted to die by explosion. There was no water in the reservoir, he explained, hence none in the boiler. What should we do, we asked. Keep out of the bathroom. But since we wanted to go into the bathroom? Well, put out the fire in the kitchen. But since we needed a fire in the kitchen? Well, arrange to get some water in the reservoir. —How? —You can't. —Then why suggest it? —Because it would be perfect if you could have water here. —Perfect? It will be necessary. —You'll never have it. —Never have it? We've rented a château with water. —You'd better examine your lease and see if it says so.

We examined our lease and came upon the exciting clause *"château loué avec l'eau."* The plumber was much interested. —*Alors,* you're within your rights, wanting water. Only there's never been water here. The people before, they put in the bathroom, they wanted water too.

And why didn't they have water?

The town hasn't enough water.

Why doesn't the town arrange to have enough water?

One can't have everything in life.

Evidently not, but one can always have water. And since the town is on a river, it seems to be asking very little . . .

He shrugged. *Que voulez-vous?*

Water! We want water!

Finally an expert mechanic suggested a solution. We could put a pump in the basement and keep the reservoir filled by pumping several hours a day. I asked if this expensive and tiresome method would absolutely guarantee water.

Absolument.

47

It wouldn't be better to buy a larger reservoir and an automatic pump?

Why? Reservoirs cost money and even then you might not have water.

Why not?

Because if the town is short of water . . .

How then will our pump help?

Well, with a hand pump you can always be sure to get any water there is.

But you just said . . .

I was forced to stop the argument as the mechanic was so incensed with my reasoning that he threatened to do nothing at all. So we decided on the pump and it was put in promptly, save for the delay caused by the death of the grandmother of the only workman who could do the job.

We found a peasant to pump and then found that pumping did no good.

It's because your conduit isn't large enough. There's no pressure.

Did you know this when you installed the pump?

You didn't ask about the conduit.

You guaranteed this pump knowing that it wouldn't function unless we changed our conduit?

Ecoutez, mademoiselle, this business will finish badly between us if you continue to talk . . .

This business began badly and has long since finished. *Partez, et partez vite!*

I sought out officials. Yes, the conduit could be

changed at a cost of 1200 francs. And we would then have water?

Mais certainement. With more pressure you're bound to have water.

You guarantee it?

Mais absolument.

Within ten days the conduit was changed and we prepared for baths. The peasant pumped for two hours; we had only a foot of water. I went back to the official.

The larger conduit does no good.

He smiled politely. But, mademoiselle, that is not surprising.

It may not be to you. To me it is shocking. It is dishonest of you to have guaranteed . . .

Pardon, mademoiselle. There is dishonesty somewhere but it is not mine. We are bringing suit against the town since they have refused to send us water. We haven't even enough for our trains. Our reservoirs are empty.

How long has this been going on?

For the last six months and . . .

You knew this when you guaranteed water?

But, mademoiselle, I never guaranteed that you would always have water. I said that a larger conduit would undoubtedly . . .

I don't remember the rest. Sometimes we had water and sometimes we hadn't. But we always had the chestnut trees. In May a cuckoo sang in them all day, in October they turned the forest into a stage-set, in December we lived within a circle of snow trees. I shall never forget the nights when, from darkened windows above, I looked down on the crescent of candlelight from *salon* windows and avenues of snow flowers in the form of a sunburst, leading through the moon-and-star-light of white elysian fields.

Of course we lost the Muette. All our book money had gone into its rental, we had nothing left. The loss was so emotionally staggering that we decided to ignore it as a reality and remember only that for two years we had lived as one rarely hopes to live; that our memory of this personally fabulous, unexpected life was permanent; no future circumstance, whatever its menace, could efface those days spent in the proportions of classic rooms, or those hours when Allen Tanner played Bach, in the *rotonde,* until the stars appeared and then played on until they set.

4. A year went by, another began. In January we were in a small hotel in the rue Jacob when Georgette was stricken with pneumonia.

At the *clinique* we sat all night outside her door. The family came, the rich half-paralyzed member heard talk of money for oxygen and found the power to move about and make determined gestures. The doctor came out of Georgette's room, smiling to hide his emotion. "She is playing her last card," he said, "and so gallantly. There is a chance for her because of that." The millionaire took him aside and murmured a request that he make his bill as low as possible. The doctor looked at him. *"Cher monsieur,"* he said, "there *is* no bill for Georgette Leblanc."

For convalescence we went to Vernet-les-Bains, in the Pyrénées Orientales. We had rented in advance a little peasant house. Everyone said we would die of loneliness, shut in among mountains and strangers. But we knew better. We arrived in the sun, in October, at the climax of an afternoon. From one side our house looked over the tiled roofs of the old town; the loggia looked toward the mountains, but we couldn't see the mountains for the grapes. They hung in blue clusters from the sky to the ground and red autumn leaves ran among the grape-vines. As I stood in happiness before them I heard Marthe Eggerth's voice singing *"Sag Mir Immer Wieder"* on a radio in the lower town.

At six o'clock I went walking. Darkness was falling over the mountains and the lanes, sheep were going home, cows were drinking at a fountain, old peasants smiled at me as they passed, the church tower had a lighted clock and broken chimes, the mountains in the distance were blue and violet, there was no sound but the cattle bells.

It was in Vernet that I first began to know and love the peasants of France. We had by this time detached ourselves more and more from the rich bourgeoisie—which I now considered a subhuman species—and begun seeing only the kind of people who pleased us. They always seemed to fall within three categories—the three rewarding human classes: artist, aristocrat, peasant . . . the first with his imposing personal world, the second with his easy

51

formal intimacy, the third with his unintimate easy formality.

Much later, during the war, we again lived in villages where our neighbors and friends were peasants. I don't know why their way of life is so pleasant, and their way of relating their life to yours so flattering. Just to know they are near is a reassurance; to know that they like you is a triumph. Their greetings are fundamental: they allow you to share their feeling that it is good—that it is a ritual—to speak of the fine day; they tell you of herbs that will cure all ills, they describe the village priest's magic in the "laying on of hands." In the evening you walk past their houses; the smoke of their pine cones perfumes the countryside, they sit in doorways and say *"Bon soir, mademoiselle"* as if they were evoking the night that will soon darken the fields; they ask you to have a *petit verre* and you drink it with a ceremony that never relaxes into casualness though you may repeat it with them a hundred times.

We were among them again at the beginning of the war, in 1940. We had a little three-room house in Le Cannet, two kilometres above Cannes. Our street, the Avenue Victoria, curved its way above the Mediterranean to the Aga Khan's villa at one end; our Chalet Rose was at the other end, with sea and distant mountains, olive trees and jasmin fields, terraced slopes of mimosa mounting toward the sky.

It was here that our visual, visible, external story came to its end.

MUCH ADO ABOUT SOMETHING

Within this outer story, like a box within a box, lies another story. Its events are more tangible to me than other realities—they are composed of the astounding life of the temperament. They are the fervors and follies and frenzies that come and go, the heights and the depths, the undefinable rapture and the unresolved despair. They are the floods of spring, the summer night. And they are the heart's delight, its gratitude and awe.

It is an anachronistic story, set in the nineteen-twenties and thirties when we all had time for personality. It is a story, first of all, about a state of happiness.

My unaccountable inner happiness has always been almost too much for me. I never had time enough to live it out, to live it down. I not only wanted to live it, years and years of it, over and over; I wanted time to think of it, over and over and over. It extended from an image of myself as a privileged person in a friendly universe down to the last drop of coffee in my cup; when I discovered more in the coffee-pot than I expected I found myself

smiling and saying, "How kind life is to me." It overwhelmed me at any moment—when I listened to music I
was sure that no other heart had ever beat so strongly
to this ecstacy.

I never sought horoscopic information as to what
favorable stars presided at my birth on November 24.
I wouldn't have been swayed by horoscopic evidence—
my confidence in universal protection went deeper than
any faith in a star. It was based on something in myself—
on a conviction that I was always creating something out
of nothing. Impressions are stronger than facts to me,
and my impression was that I was one of the world's most
favored beings, lifted through space from one rapturous
event to another, possessing everything necessary for happiness and living like a lighted Christmas tree. The facts
are that I have never "possessed" anything—beautiful objects, properties, money, security, peace. I have never been
able to move about the planet with freedom, as I should
love to do; I have never perfected any natural gift, I have
never acquired knowledge I should love to have; I have
never become what I would wish to be. But the impression
persisted: "I am so happy, I have always been so desper-
ately happy." ("As unhappy as that?" Orage * said. But
this was much later—when, after years and years of loving my life and fighting against losing it, I realized that
my exemption must end, that I must one day sit down upon
the ground.)

Of course this happy story might have taken place
anywhere, as well as in France. It is a story of life on a

* A. R. Orage, the English editor, who appears later in this book.

cloud. And though there is no better *mise-en-scene* for such a life than France, I realize that any country will serve for the silver-lined events of a self-shaped story.

As I look at the human story I see two stories. They run parallel and never meet. One is of people who live, as they can or must, the events that arrive; the other is of people who live, as they intend, the events they create. The first category would have been impossible for me.

I have never been able to take a serious part in the events that seem chiefly to engage mankind—making wars, making laws, making money. This situation looked to me like a status-quo world; no movement seemed possible for me within its orbit, and the orbit seemed likely to stay fixed. I don't yet see any interest in this world, and I have been so blest as never to have been drawn into it. I never lived in a country that ordered its women to war, and no one whose life was vital to me (oh supreme dispensation!) ever had to go to war; I couldn't make money, but my friends have always invited me to share their money in exchange for sharing my world; I couldn't make laws, and laws haven't the slightest interest for me—except in the world of science, in which they are always changing; or in the world of art, in which they are unchanging; or in the world of Being in which they are, for the most part, unknown.

Of course I have always been told that if all people were like me the world wouldn't progress. I found this as misleading as everything else I was told. First because they aren't like me, second because they wouldn't like to be. They are interested in the problems and prescriptions of the status-quo world. They would be utterly bored to be like me. And who am I to say that they are wrong? But aren't they, since they are always worried and at war?

Next, I was told that I would discover life to be different from what I imagined it to be. I never made this discovery. Life for me has been exactly what I thought it would be—a cake, which I have eaten and had too. I was born a happy person in the shelter of an easy "fate." Until a few years ago I never looked straight at any fact except my capacity to make a happy life a happier one; and I have always been able to draw my friends into this arrangement. Happiness to me meant: appreciation of what you have; anticipation of what you plan to have, whether you ever have it; gratitude that you are not in competition for what others have, or want to have; the capacity to ignore what you don't like, or to turn it into what you do like; and the surpassing reward of finding that you can really believe in what you hoped you could believe in.

Naturally I have had hardships, but I thought they were illusions. They must have been, since I can't remember them. I'm sure I never had a real hardship. I have never been wounded or put into a concentration camp. I have never had to sleep under a bridge or stand in a bread line. I have never been too hungry or too tired, too ill or too cold, too ugly or too wrong, too crowded or too alone. I have never been bored or disabled, really depressed or really discouraged. I have never had to live in friction or misunderstanding; when they arrived I departed. I have never felt youth diminishing or age approaching. I have never been *too* hurt. I have been too bereaved, but what I lost was a love too deep to diminish. Therefore I knew from the beginning that though death taketh all away, *this* he could not take.

My basic happiness was founded on this fact—this unmatchable fact: that one sometimes finds a human being with whom one can have a true and limitless human communication. The words for this blessing are "love," or "understanding," or the exact word the French have for it —an *"entente."*

This is the first of the two real events I spoke of: finding some one about whom I felt at once—as if a prophecy were being made to me—"There is something perfect in her soul."

For twenty-one years I never saw Georgette Leblanc do anything, never heard her say anything, that did not spring from this perfection. It is a quality, I think, that arises in the creative mind. Putting my trust in this quality, I felt that whatever I might be, the best of me (or even the worst) would never be misunderstood by Georgette. It never was. She always made me feel that there was something perfect in *me*. I could never be grateful enough for this distinction. Since she believed it, it must be so. As long as she lived, I felt that I was always smiling.

I often tried to steady my breathless and conscious happiness over this *entente* by trying to name those perfections in Georgette which made a friendship with her a story never to be forgotten. I would wonder in what order to name them—which one took precedence in her golden-ruled life: goodness, wisdom, understanding, courage, humility, humanity, intelligence, aspiration . . . Combined with secondary traits like tact, grace, charm, courtesy, ardor, humor, imagination, justice, reasonableness, freedom . . . I realize that I am describing her as a paragon. But she *was* a paragon—even her "faults" underlined the fact. She had many vanities, but no *amour-propre;* she was self-absorbed, but never selfish; she was naïve, but not childish—she was child-like; she had an anxiety-complex, but with a manner that redeemed it; she had the electricity of temper, but she used it abstractly, not personally; she often lacked judgment, but always constructively; and she had an ego that never behaved egotistically. Perhaps I could assemble her qualities under one major tendency: personal distinction, aristocracy of nature—in other words that greatest, to me, of all human attributes: an unspoiled heart; in clearer words, a psyche that has none of the poisons that most psyches accumulate during their lifetime of self-vindication. As a consequence she had many enemies—just as Maeterlinck became her enemy: she was too good to be true. But Georgette was no one's enemy.

Most lives lived under the same roof intrude, impose, infringe, impinge upon each other. Georgette would never have impinged upon a bird, certainly not upon a fellow creature. The space she lived in made her assume that you too wanted space; she never commented upon your behavior since that would restrict your space. She objected even to mild comment—the kind that ruffles or surprises or disperses. The kind most people indulge in—

the comment that disturbs, distresses, baffles, irritates, de-
presses, angers, wounds—filled her with horror. As to
temper, she was far too tempered to understand its need
or use as an involuntary explosion. It would have been
as impossible for her to speak to anyone "in a temper"
as it would have been for her to shoot him, swiftly and
unreasonably, in the temple. A display of temper between
two friends seemed to her a vulgarity so harsh and final
as to leave them forever estranged, their relationship reduced to the illogicality of that between a man and a wild
beast. To Georgette there was no human conflict, between
friends, which couldn't be resolved by a glance between
understanding eyes.

Even the milder human idiosyncracies seemed to her
to be rooted in vulgarity. No one could ever imagine her
making a disagreeable remark, or expressing any of the
other clichés of daily living that seem acceptable to most
people. In all the years I never heard her say anything
like "What's the matter with you?" She never felt free to
say to anyone "I know what's the matter," "You must be
nervous," "Aren't you being disagreeable?" "There's no
use talking," "I wouldn't say it if it weren't true" . . .
etc., etc., etc., etc. To Georgette these attacks on another
person's inner world could be made only in an outer
world of which she knew nothing. I once made a list of
sixty-five remarks of this type which I never heard her
make. When anyone said, "But it's natural for people to
talk like that to one another," she said it seemed as anti-
natural to her as the freaks in a circus.

She might say "I was a little worried because you're

late"; she would never say "You worry me by being late," "Why do you worry me by being late?" "Why are you late?" "You shouldn't be late," "I hate it that you're late," "Can't you be on time?" Her comments were never criticism; if she had criticism to make she made it with style, as in a written essay. Her comments were not grievance, habit, compensation, involuntary expression, automatic monitorship, unconscious pleasure, or a means of communication. They were not based on the assumption that any human being is answerable to another, that any human being ever really understands another. She didn't comment, she created.

The kinds of thing she did say were simple things, but source things. They were the things said by a person who has made much life. They always made me feel that I was being informed, inspired, soothed or saved. She once described someone's life by saying, *"C'est une vie qui parle avec des gens."* Of our lives she said, *"C'est toujours comme si quelque chose arrivait."* Defining a special grace she felt in someone's presence, she said, *"C'est comme si toute une vie harmonieuse venait vers moi"*; defining the two-dimensional quality of another person's life,—*"Il me semble que je prends le thé avec un chien"*; describing the slowness of another person's responses—*"Elle semble attendre au bout d'un corridor"*; analyzing someone's egotism—*"Vanité—pire espèce: celle qui affiche son humilité."* Once she went to call upon someone whose apartment faced a cemetery—*"Ah!"* she said, *"quelle joie! tous ces gens qui ne parlent pas."* Once she described a friend as having *"adorabilite d'etre."* But

"adorability of being" should be her own description, because her mind and heart were of gentle birth.

This was the *entente* in which I lived and breathed;
this was the harmonic scale in which I felt that all things
of life and art and mind were understood. Take everything
else from me, I used to say, but leave me this one com-
munion and I will have a total life. I always wanted it
more than anything else, I found it, I never found a flaw
in it, I never stopped being grateful for it. I remember
being grateful every day, moment after moment during
the days during the years, as if I must express gratitude
aloud to myself. I would find myself saying at almost any
moment: to live without Georgette's delicacy would be to
find the world an alien place; I should miss too much her
"being at home with everything but the normal"; I should
miss too much her way of laughing; perhaps I should miss
more than anything else the way she said *"C'est abom-
inable"*—I should not know where to turn for the comfort
of her stupefaction over human buffoonery, her blasting
and warming and inclusive indictment of the stupidities of
the human species. But most of all I knew I would miss
the way she said *"C'est trop beau."*

Sometimes I tried to decide which story about her
would best illustrate her nature. Perhaps this one:

Once when she was ill we spent the winter in a mountain village where the air was pure. One day she was sitting in bed beside her Christmas tree, already a month
old. It was snowing and the windows were open. A little
bird flew in—a winter sparrow. It flew close to her and
settled on a branch of the Christmas tree. "There it in-

stalled itself," she said, "as if it were *chez lui*. I loved its visit, I wanted to do something *aimable* for him, but we simply looked at each other. *Longtemps nous sommes restés ainsi.*"

It was in this village, Vernet-les-Bains, that we spent some of our most iridescent days. Our peasant house had a little living-room papered in midnight blue, where we gathered on winter afternoons before the hottest stove I have ever known, while snowflakes rushed at the mountains. And there was a low dark dining-room papered in fruits and flowers where Georgette drew cartoons that kept us laughing all winter. I love to laugh all kinds of laughter, but there is one kind that pleases me more than others. It is the helpless kind; not as you laugh at wit but as you laugh at comedy. I have more fun with funniness than with wittiness, more pleasure in humor than in epigrams, just as I have more interest in personal report than in erudition. These cartoons were personal reports of Georgette's fun with two worlds—ourselves and "people." We were still explaining the difference between ourselves and those others with whom we never felt at home. We talked a lot about these distinctions in Vernet, as the days enclosed us in a valley and our molehills became mountains.

One day Georgette formulated what she considered the difference between us and intellectuals. We live for emotions, she said, they live for events. In our relations with people we wait upon the development of personal atmosphere; they don't wait, they crouch. This crouching embarrasses our intelligence; the crouchers are like cats before a mouse-hole. "Why don't they just sit down in a chair and exist?" she said. "They aren't content to do this, they have an avidity, they don't want to talk to people in order to know them, but only to learn something from them. They become critics. Nothing ever happens in the presence of the little critic. A person of genius may be boring—he has his jokes and his stories; but all this is compensated for by the flavor of his presence, which sooner or later penetrates the situation. With people it's the same as with poetry—bulk is necessary: every poem is not a gem. I like people who are like good fruits—much juice. I couldn't live in an atmosphere uncharged with personal existence. Writers can't write in the midst of every-day life; I can't exist in the midst of every-day vibrations."

After our conversations I would go walking in the evening, past the muted fountain and the lighted church, through the silent hills. Sometimes the village people told me it would snow in the high mountains that night; we could feel the snow waiting to fall. Then we would dine surrounded by fruits and flowers on peasant walls, we would open the windows toward the distant snow, the valleys were full of lights like stars. When I went upstairs Georgette would be singing Honneger's "Adieu," with the heartbreaking words by Apollinaire:*

> *J'ai cueilli ce brin de bruyère*
> *L'automne est morte, souviens t'en*
> *Nous ne nous verrons plus sur terre*

* From *Alcools—Poèmes 1898-1913*, by Guillaume Apolinaire. Published by the Nouvelle Revue Française, Paris.

LANDSCAPE WITH FIGURES

Odeur du temps, brin de bruyère
Et souviens-toi que je t'attends.

I stood in the door to listen and said goodnight as after
an event. At midnight I wakened and turned on the radio.
Waltzes from Frankfurt. I looked out the window—a
mountain, a cloud, a star, a waltz on earth . . .

This was my daily life year after year. No one has
ever told me of living in an equal uninterrupted felicity.
Perhaps no one else would enjoy it. I don't understand
why not. I always hoped for it and I found it. This was
the blue skies and white clouds of all my days.

2. Another reason for my ubiquitous happiness was my vanity. To begin with, I liked myself—
liked the way I behaved, the way I thought and felt, the
way I looked—except for certain obvious defects which
with intelligence, labor and discomfort I could disguise.
I disliked certain characteristics—for one, my way of living in italics. I had too much to say and used too many
words to say it; I wished I had the dignity to say nothing
or the poise to say something focused and clear. But, in
all seriousness of vanity, I liked myself because as a
human statement I could give myself an almost unquali-
fied approval. I was glad never to have felt underhanded,
never to have needed double motives or to have advanced
behind defense mechanisms (I thought); glad to know that
never in my life had I said anything to anyone in anger
that I couldn't later repeat and find to be coherent, àpro-

pos, measured, just. These virtues not only pleased me, they gave me a ruling attitude—with divine rights and privileges.

All this made me a dictator. I could win all arguments because I could prove that the artist always wins over the intellectual; on the other hand, I could prove that the intensities of temperament (which I loved) must be subjected to the mind's discriminations (which I loved more); I could convince the religionist that he must incorporate science, and the scientist that he must comprehend super-science; I could demonstrate that knowledge must always bow to understanding; I could force everyone to respect the exaltations; I could even give form to that formless thing, romantic love; I could arrange all elements into the proper pictures, I could produce composition on all sides; I could edit life as I would edit a manuscript, to extract the quintessence of its yield.

Such a person lives on the conviction of always being right. I thought I knew the difference between right and wrong, good and bad, that I had an infallible judgment of what was "most" moving or beautiful or interesting. Many people hated me for this but I couldn't see why. If I said that Art has been present in the cinema on only four or five occasions—in "Caligari," in "The Beggars' Opera" (German), in Olivier's Shakespeare, in Disney's "Old Mill," in one moment of "Odd Man Out"— my statement might be true, why was it antagonistic? If someone said it wasn't true I wasn't antagonized, I was excited, I wanted to hear his proof, I would withdraw mine if his could carry me away. I didn't understand why people wanted to strike me because I said such things. It would be more logical for me to go about striking people because they didn't say them—because they said less interesting things. But many people have no standards of interest. I had always thought that such standards were as definite as standards of time in music. But years ago— the strain of the memory is with me still—I went to a concert with someone who said "What a lovely waltz movement" when the orchestra was playing a movement in 4/4 time. I said, "It's not a waltz, it's 4/4." She said, "No, 3/4." I said, "4/4—beat it out and you'll see." She beat a few measures vaguely. I took her hand and made it beat precisely. She said, "No, it's 3/4." I said, "I will go mad if you can't hear it right." It *was* 4/4—I showed her the score afterward.

I always felt that I knew the score. From morning till night I lived like an orchestra conductor. My bed always faced the light so that I felt in command of my room. My first sensation when I woke was of reaching for a baton. Breakfast was already on my bed-table. I lighted the alcohol lamp and while the coffee heated I looked about—first at nature, to judge the day and decide what plan was imposed by sun, rain, wind or snow; then at our personal world to decide which plight took precedence over others. Almost no events took place but everything that did take place was an event to me. And I wanted my events planned. There was something so attractive to me in plans that I applied them even to moods. I used to say, *"Now* let's be interesting," or *"Now* let's be amusing." This usually had a dampening effect on everyone except Jane Heap who also loved plans and was never so amusing as by design. Plans offer arrangement and I had discovered that arrangement was the elixir above all others that stimulated my glands; organization— of objects, situations, places, people, pleasure, work, ideas.

Order is life to me. I could, if necessary, live in dirt but never in disorder. A place for everything and everything in its place—this is only the beginning of it. *What* places? Not arrangement in any or all ways, but arrangement in certain ways. Everything bears a relation to everything else, the eye travels from left to right, order may be defined as "objects vibrating in harmony," the laws are important and must be kept. Georgette, who revered disorder, said that to live as I did would make her feel she was living the life of a doll. "Curious," I said, "instead of a doll I feel like Bach. He said, 'The order which rules music is the same order that controls the placing of the stars and the feathers in a bird's wing—it is essential and eternal. Nothing was ever created in disorder—the chaotic and unfinished are against the laws of the spirit. I like to feel myself in the middle of the harmony.' "

Form living—this is what I want. I like to eliminate confusion from life as I do from a house. Sometimes I reduce my room to chaos, until my muscles ache to begin its reconstruction, plan it all out again, set it in order, turn it into form. At the end I feel that I have created a world. Why not? A planned universe, a planned room— plans begin at home. My plans have made me aware of rhythm in all things, kept me from feeling like a star wandering from its course, preserved me from life's most dire formlessness—domesticity.

The laws of order are unalterable, perhaps this is why they are the only delightful laws. There are no two sides to the question, there is confusion or order, chaos or—a choice, a distinction, a proof, a crusade. There is a phrase I dislike—"law and order." I never use it, to me it has no sense; it should be changed to "the laws of order." You can't talk about law without antagonizing me. Human laws are full of holes—what is good one day, in one place, is bad in another. I like my laws airtight. Like seven days in a week, or the cart behind the horse.

If I were to compose ten definitions of order I should do it like this:

1. A plan for everything and everything in its plan.
2. A plan recognized by other planners.
3. One good plan leading to another.
4. A study in conception.
5. The organization of relations.
6. The conditions of creation.
7. Arrangement à propos.
8. The octave.
9. Dancing.
10. Church architecture for week days.

And I have another mania about order which no one seems to respect as I do. I am always disturbed when someone catches me on the wing and asks me if I don't want to do something. I want to answer: "I never *want* to do anything, at any time, except to continue what I am already doing until I have finished it."

I have never lived in a room that wasn't a still-life—
I couldn't. There is a certain country house where I love
to go but it has an uncomposed room where I always feel
distressed. There is a table in it so badly placed that I
can't keep my mind off it, I never know quite what I am
saying or doing or what anyone else is talking about
because of that break in the wall where the table should
stand at right angles. I want to get my hands on it. Then
the long room would fall into order and I could win my
chess games.

Organization—this is the call of the wild to me.
Interior decoration should have been my fixation but I
find more exultation in rearranging a room than in creating a new one. I have no flair for choosing materials—
I know very little about their quality or powers. I have
no passion of touch, I can't stand fingering silks or velvet,
all I want is to take objects in my hands and place them
where they belong. I never walk into a strange room without at a glance replacing everything in it where it should
be. I should love to be a professional prescriber—a house
doctor. Give me an old house full of old things and I
will give it new life through arrangement. Line rather
than color, design rather than material. I never watch
people studying materials without feeling that they are
wasting time; but I will spend hours over a seam in a
coat feeling that I am engaged in a relation, however
remote, to the laws of the universe.

Georgette always said, "I have no order but I have *care*."
She never broke objects or wore them out, she never de-

stroyed anything, especially old papers. Nothing would induce her to tear up a letter, she even saved the address slips around newspapers, you could find them lying about in her room weeks later. In the scale between brutality and delicacy there existed for her a note that she named (to my confusion) sensitiveness. She would say, *"Je suis très sensible."* Now there is no word in the French language I distrust more than *sensible*. Every time I hear it I brace myself for some climax of physical disaster. One day Georgette was explaining to me her dreary distinctions between "care" and "order," her gift for preservation and conservation. "Now take this butter," she began. I said, "If I'm to take the butter I'll take it out of the bedroom." "You don't understand, *cherie*," she said, "you don't know the difference between good and bad butter." "What's the butter doing in the bedroom?—that's all I want to understand," I said. She explained: it is difficult, in any country, to find superlative butter; once you have found it you must take care of it. We had no ice-box at the lighthouse and this exceptional butter which had come up on her breakfast tray deserved exceptional treatment. "You'll be surprised," she said, "to see what an ingenious plan I've found." I said I wouldn't be surprised and I wouldn't call it a plan. She had put the butter in water, in a glass dish. She led me to a closet door and opened it with pride. The water and the butter had been carefully placed in the crown of a hat and another large garden hat placed over them as a protection against microbes.

Georgette was especially ingenious about her traveling arrangements in the car and felt that I was too inflexible in mine. But I never saw the necessity for ingenuity, I just wanted the bags placed side by side. After several savage experiences in the Citroên between Paris and Cannes I decided to make a list of those objects and atmospheres I could accept and those I must refuse. I drew up the paper formally with a dotted line on which we were all to sign. I felt that my restrictions showed a wide margin of flexibility.

Invitation au voyage

I accept the invitation with pleasure
I also accept:

>   delays
>   changes of plan
>   lack of plans
>   fantasies (I hate them)
>   catastrophes (I expect them)
>   too much air
>   too little air
>   cold
>   heat
>   rain
>   snow
>   a monotonous sun
>   bad food
>   bad service
>   bad butter
>   bad beds
>   dirt (in any sympathetic environment)
>   unsympathetic environments
>   confusion
>   isolation

lost routes
wrong directions
unexpected destinations
lack of baths
lack of food
lack of precisions
lack of decisions
lack of formalities
domesticities
complaints against the climate
complaints against anything
regrets that time flies
regrets that the car doesn't
dissatisfactions with the trip
reactions of all types

I refuse to accept:

Fantasies (confusion) of luggage.

1. I ask that all *articles de voyage* shall be contained in a *sac de voyage.*

2. I refuse to discover, placed on the floor of the car or jolting about in the rumble seat:
alcohol lamps
empty (or filled) bottles
pots of jam
iodine
food in paper bags
shoes
sugar
pillows
furniture
crumbs
medicines
newspaper clippings

packages in newspapers
hot water bottles
writing paper
thermometers
flowers
honey
animals of all types (taken along or welcomed en route)

3. I refuse to send half the luggage by train, not being interested in waiting for it, losing it, looking for it in stations where it will never be, or hearing about luggage checks which should but can't be found.

4. I refuse to get into the car if the luggage bulges from the windows.

We all signed the paper and everything turned out as usual. I didn't mind of course. I could stand physical disasters because, with Georgette, I never had to stand mental or emotional ones. In spite of her religion of dis-order, she had an absolute formality about the manner of one's communal living: concentration, privacy, no casual talk, no thinking out loud, no singing in the bathroom. We lived with form. Anything else would have seemed to us like living in a house in which all the doors are always open.

I have a story about this dire and informal domestic attitude:

It began on a formal spring morning when I drove to Dieppe to meet a friend coming from London. We had planned a trip in the Citroên and had corresponded about luggage, deciding that the car would harmoniously accept four small bags of hers and my own four. I had asked her to

leave her umbrella at home and to bring instead a special
Bach record. My plan was that she would step off the night
boat, step into the car, we would drive to the Royal for
coffee and *croissants* in the early morning with mist over
the sea front, we would talk of the charm of this phenomenon, then step into the car in the carefree mood appropriate
to an approach to Munich, Salzburg, Vienna. I knew the
car would spare us the confusion of tire trouble, I knew
my four highly-organized bags in the rumble would spare
me the confusion of wandering objects, and I drove to the
quai confident that in my well-managed house-car no domestic crisis could arise. My friend was also an efficient
person, she had always told me, with scorn for people who
don't manage to "get enough things done" in life.

She stepped off the boat and I saw the umbrella. She
said, handing it to me, "Isn't it awful, I forgot the Bach."
I said, "That's too bad, we can leave it at the hotel." She
said, "Do you think it will be safe?" I said, "I'm afraid
so." She laughed but not conspicuously. "It's a Briggs
umbrella, it cost a fortune." "Why didn't you leave it in
your safe?" I said. We put it in the car. Now I realize that
umbrellas are to the English what web feet are to ducks
and geese—nature's equipment for the environment; but
I knew we wouldn't need that umbrella in a romantic city
like Vienna, I knew I never needed to see it again in any
city.

The porter placed five deep and heavy bags beside the
umbrella and we started for the Royal. She said, "What a
lovely morning, I've quite a few things to do before we
start." "Let's do them later," I said, "when we're tired of

driving." "Oh no," she said, "they must be posted from here." She was in high spirits.

We ordered coffee and *croissants* in the glass restaurant. The sea was probably wonderful but we didn't look at it. She said she had brought a present for Georgette but hadn't wrapped it because she wanted me to see it first. It was lovely but I have never cared much for it, it remains an object I was forced to look at when I wanted to look at the sea. She had brought tissue paper to wrap it in, and ribbon, but we had to send the concierge in search of wrapping-paper. Then she asked me to address the package. I had to address it in ink, which I haven't used for years. I don't like ink on my fingers, I always use colored crayons for packages but my crayons were at home in a desk drawer where they belonged. Then we sent the concierge for string, there is never any string in a French hotel. He had to send a garçon to a distant shop for it, then I had to wrap the package. I hate wrapping packages as much as I hate touching string, it puckers my fingers and they had been feeling so smooth on the wheel. There was no way of weighing the package because, though the concierge had a weighing-machine, he hadn't one large enough for this large package. "Put a lot of stamps on it and trust to luck," I said. "Oh no," she said, "I like to do things properly." I left her and the concierge to work it out together and went to sit in an armchair.

I had just begun to rest when I heard her say, "Ah, there you are." She had another package in her hand, a smaller one. It contained a piece of jewelry that was broken. She had a special jeweler in Paris who always mended her jewels and she wanted me to write him a note in French telling him what to do. I said, "Why, oh why, didn't you send it from London?" knowing the answer in advance. She spoke at some length on custom duties, then said, "But just a little note, so easy for you." My easy chair stood beside a writing-table, there was no escaping the easiness of the situation. The pen was broken and there was no writing-paper on the table but we easily remedied this and I began the letter. If there is anything I loathe to do more than write a letter in French, I can't think of it now nor could I then. My French has no appeal in writing, nor have I any such ambition for it, nor do I care what M. Cartier thought of that letter, but I do care about a spring morning—enough to write my letters in French (if any) on a rainy autumn afternoon. We went again to the concierge's desk, bought a stamp, asked him to mail the letter promptly, and gave him the package to weigh—it was small enough this time for the machine. Then she sent some telegrams—I had sent mine as telegrams should be sent, when one is alone. She asked me, for efficiency's sake, to address hers while she composed. Thus we gained some time. She paid for the telegrams, with confusions about the exchange from English into French money, and remarked that she must soon get some more money out of her bags.

There was one more thing to do . . . the umbrella. She looked the concierge in the eye and asked him if he were a man to be trusted. He was frightened but said yes. She took him into her confidence about the umbrella. Her French was halting but she wanted him to realize that this umbrella was English. I tried to translate these confidences, stripped to essentials, into efficient French, but she waved me off, she wanted to put the weight of her personality behind her words. The concierge, intimidated, promised to guard the umbrella as his very eyes.

Then we got into the car. Still convinced that all was pleasant and normal she sank into her seat and said with enthusiasm that she wouldn't really feel we had started on our trip until we had passed the German frontier. As Strasbourg was five hundred kilometres away and I was two hours less near it than I had planned to be, I didn't find my usual response to this challenge. After an hour, as we were driving past fields, she asked me to stop so that she could get into her valises for money. I stopped the car. She said, "I'm afraid you'll have to help me." I had been afraid of this for some time. I reached for the bag on top. "No," she said, "we'll have to get to the bottom one." So I got to it. I took off my topcoat and pulled out five monumental bags. I would have liked to find some strong field laborer for this work but the fields were empty. The bags bumped and scraped over my new seat covers. She gave me the keys to the bottom one which hadn't one lock but two; then I strained and bumped the bags back into the car.

We rode on. I sensed that she was becoming aware of my silence, suspecting at last that all was not pleasant. She said, "I don't think you're being very sporting." I said, "I don't see any sport." She said, "One has to do a lot of things in life one doesn't enjoy." "You must phrase it differently," I said, "you mean: one must manage to get a lot of things done."

A month later we were back in Dieppe. We went to the

Royal for lunch but really for the umbrella. The concierge was still there but he hadn't guarded the umbrella as his very eyes. He still had his eyes, but he. . . . You know the rest.

The Unseeing Eye

The important thing to discover about one's manias is not only their cause but what state they cause in you. Mine have often put me in a state of dangerous frenzy, and just as often I have written a paper about it—for all to see.

Once we had a guest who made me ill with her disorder and the paper I wrote was called "The Unseeing Eye":

When tragedies happen to you, I can *see* them, therefore I can understand them. You can't see mine, therefore they don't exist for you.

One of the most wearing of my tragedies is that I am forced, every time I enter a room where a careless person has been living, to trace the visible passage of that carelessness on every object —the train of hideous displacements: socks, shoes, clothes, letters, empty envelopes, pens, pencils, food in conjunction with lip rouge, hairpins, combs lying beside orange peels . . . forced to see a picture of the brain-life that can leave such traces, that can live within their horror—the traces of an unconsciously-offending animal . . . forced to torment myself with the knowledge that they will continue throughout your life, that you will meet tragic situations because of them and never be able to trace the tragedies to their source, any more than you can see or trace the odious octave of your physical disorder.

As to my own relation to this tragedy, I know that you will continue these offenses as long as I know you, in spite of any-

thing I can say or do, in spite of all the special pleading I have
sent out. I have used every means, from the most subtle hints,
pictures, examples, to the most drastic descriptions of my suffering. You now know what real pain this sloth causes me. You will
do *nothing* to alleviate it. The fact that you won't is a deep dis-
courtesy; it has the effect of a deliberate affront.

Even if you suspect my suffering you probably consider it
merely neurotic. Perhaps it is fundamental; I think it is since it
causes me to be estranged from you. I don't want to be estranged,
I resent your forcing me to be. For one reason alone I think you
should try to preserve me from this alienation: for the sake of
everyone concerned I hate to be more ugly than I need to be:
my face—its very features—depends upon harmony; during these
days of brooding obsession on the idea of sloth, I am ashamed
of the ugliness of my iron face; I want to hide it from everyone;
it must give you a dull aesthetic pain to look at such a face. But
perhaps you don't even see it.

You are living in a house which we created as a place of
beauty and comfort. To turn it into a slums is an affront. The
awful aspect of this tragedy is that you could so easily correct it.
You are only twenty; you could change your habits as easily as
you change your clothes. But you do not WISH to. It is all nothing to you—because of what you are not able to see.

The tragedy of unawareness extends into many realms. As
you are unaware of your presence in a room, of its unconscious
manifestations—completely unaware of how your body acts, unaware of your feet on the brocaded chair—so are you unaware of
what you do walking along a street, riding in a taxi: you hum
and sing beside me while I quiver with nerves. You are so unaware of my emanations that you don't know they are flowing
toward you with strangling force. IS IT AN ADVANTAGE IN
LIFE TO BE SO UNAWARE? And why are you? We have
often talked about humming, whistling, singing, as the automatic
and undesirable manifestations of an unconscious animal. Don't

you WANT to remember that they are unbearable to people trying to live with some degree of consciousness?

Once in your presence I tapped with my fingers on a table
in time to music on the radio. Within five seconds you said:
"Please don't do that, it makes me nervous." I said, "Of course,
sorry," and stopped. Have I ever done it since in your presence?
Not once. I may have other manifestations that are trying—you
have only to tell me so; with all my force, with all my memory,
I will always try to remember not to make that gesture when I
am with you. It shouldn't be an overwhelming strain on any organism to turn this manifestation on and off at will. WISH and
WILL—two great words. To live without such impulses is to live
a sub-life, a life that excludes a process known as evolution.

Art

Among my other discriminations—standards of behavior, standards of emotion—was my uncompromising
attitude toward Art.

I remember an argument I once had with a singer.
I would describe her as a person who in speaking, smiling,
breathing, walking, feeling, touching, tasting, talking,
doesn't know the difference between rhythm and jerking.
She insisted that she was an artist. "What makes you think
so?" I said. "Because I sing, I give concerts." "Proving
what?" I said. "Well, you've never heard me sing," she
said. "I don't need to hear you sing," I said—"you
couldn't be an artist, you haven't got the face-expression."[*]

Art to me was a state, it didn't need to be an accom-
plishment. By any of the standards of production, achieve-
ment, performance, I was not an artist. But I always
thought of myself as one. Ah, the religion I have been able

80 [*] This last phrase was said to myself.

to feel toward the art of music as it is played on pianos. I so loved my own way of playing that I never found the stamina for professional practice. I could work endless hours on music I already played to perfection, but I was incapable of a concentrated hour over Mozart or others who offered me no abiding-place for my emotions. I never studied harmony—the emotions don't need to study harmony. I see that I never had any intention of becoming a pianist. I just wanted to listen to music. My years passed in this swoon.

The years of Georgette's life passed in this same fainting and rejoicing. When she sang she communicated "the state"—people remembered after thirty years her conception of a song.

To me the indication of Art resides in the speaking, singing, playing, writing, of a single phrase. Art-expression. What is it? A presentation of something. Of what? Of a *conception*. But what is a conception? And a conception of *what?*

There can be an obsession in the mind's search for a definition; one is besieged by the necessity for precision.

When you feel the presence of the element of conception, you are lifted outside yourself—beyond detail, dialectic, document—beyond all that is informing into what is overpowering; you have been impregnated—simultaneously, permanently—with every factor of the created thing; you have been given a distillation, in one final formula, of the idea. The stamp of super-knowledge has been put upon it—you can't go any higher with any added findings—you have got the full meaning, the final, unequalled,

81

unsurpassable interpretation. You have been endowed.

If I think of Schubert I think like this: One day he was overpowered by an emotion of love. I "see" his feeling about his emotion—it's as if he had taken it up in his hands and held it toward someone, toward something. It was an offering. The higher he held it the finer became the distillation—down to its essence, up to its yield . . . four notes . . . ta-ta-ta-*ta* . . . a serenade—the essence of serenade; the offering was gratitude—that, to him, such a feeling of love had been presented; he was endowed with it. So the "Serenade" was made on a conception of gratitude? Perhaps. I don't know. I know that I went into a café at evening, after a day of listening to people talk of love and pity and compassion. I was worn out because I couldn't make them see that they had no love, no pity, certainly no compassion; that they were expressing self-love and grievance and (as the highest they could reach) toleration. I sat down at the café table and leaned on it and put my head against my hand. And then a radio played the Schubert "Serenade." I raised my head, I leaned back against the bench, I looked up and saw a cloud pass in the sky. I was awed; I was overpowered.

So the "Serenade" was made on a conception of what is love, as against what isn't? I think so. Like right and wrong? Yes, I believe I have always thought this way about Art.

The Art of Life

Sometimes at night when I am tired, when I have spent the day, fiercely against my will and wish, watching a long parade of the *bêtises humaines,* I soothe myself by picturing their antidotes. I substitute for all ordinary human actions the sublime ones which might have taken their place; I pick and choose among my memories those luminous pictures of human behavior that I have watched so attentively; I linger over those moments of kindness so real, of understanding so deep, that I am able to banish the monstrosity of "people's" conduct toward one another and I can fall peacefully to sleep.

But on other days I am not a detached spectator of the monstrosities. Sometimes, for the thousandth time, I can't resist fighting them. I begin by explanation, arrive at pomposity, and finish in frenzy. Sometimes I become dangerous with enraged electricity; my eyes burn or freeze and I turn them away from people, fearing that my glance will burn or freeze them. My eyes behave this way when I must watch what I do not admire. At these moments I realize that I cannot live through these matters *without* my spirit blazing; I also realize that I cannot live *with* my eyes blazing. So I revert to my childhood solution: to calm myself and my eyes I write a paper expressing my rebellion and my ideas. I believe that everyone will yearn to read it. I stay up all night, unconscious of the hours that pass—a solitary, brooding, seething human organism sitting under a strong light and typing hundreds of words which I believe should enflame the world.

And what is it all about? It is a disturbance over right and wrong again. I want something created and maintained —an art of life. I am disturbed because this state is not prevalent.

"What is your leading passion?" someone asked at dinner. I said, "A passion for ideas." Someone else said, "I have a passion for proper human behavior."

"Oh, I too," I said—"but not the usual codes. You object to all that is not 'right' according to a simple subjective code: a 'man' does this, a 'cad' does that; a rough uncivilized person does this, a 'gentleman' does that."

I object to all the codes; in fact I object to all human behavior. There is something about it that won't justify you in being yourself; there is something about it that causes people to leave home. I did leave home for that reason. I went in search of a place in which, or a person with whom, I could be myself. I am glad I did. I was always a moralist and I had a high conception of life as an art.

Of course life-as-an-art is a lost cause. Why so much of my life has been spent in lost causes is difficult to explain. Except that they are not lost, for me, since I have lived so many of them with vitality and delight.

The Art of Love

In real love you want the other person's good. In romantic love you want the other person.

But even the light and lovely subject of romantic love has its laws and should be an art.

Romantic love has always seemed to me unaccountable, unassailable, unforgettable, and nearly always unattainable. I know I have found it only twice, in all its perfection, yet I feel that I have always been engaged in it—as if it were something that must always reappear, like leaves on trees. I suppose I am among those people who

84

have always been, and rarely are, in love. Perhaps that is why I was sure I knew so much about it.

Once, a long time ago, and never to be forgotten, and apart from all other love or in-loveness or love of love, I fell in love. My plans for this love contained more "conception" than is usual even in such a veteran planner as myself. It was to have been such a well-directed dream that no one, especially the dreamers, would ever quite have known what it was all about. I had planned to live years and years of mystery.

Love, I had always felt, is so human that you can't see the love for the humanness. I was going to change all this. There was to be no human nature in my plan, nothing daily or reasonable—just the astounding power of the love-potion. Nothing would ever happen that couldn't be mistaken for a dream. Everything would take on the unreality appropriate to "love"—a thing that comes from nowhere, no one knows why; that goes as it comes, no one knows where. I was born to a willing rôle in this lovely miasma, and life as I have lived it has only tended to perfect a natural talent for walking in sleep. I live without memory of facts, or of how stories end. I remember everything I have ever felt, every phrase that has ever touched my mind. I can't remember the date of my birth, only the dates of my emotions. I really don't know how old I am—the numerals of my birth year began to get mixed up with other peoples' numerals and since then I have lived in agelessness.

Another thing I easily forgot is that there are people who divide love into categories, who respect certain categories and condemn others. Of course, when I remember to remember, I realize that such people exist somewhere, but my separation from them is geographical; they can't exist in my climate and landscape. I used to know all kinds of people with all kinds of ideas. I fought with them, but that was long ago. Now I know only serious people. I can't imagine any of them commenting on romantic love except to say "Ah?"

I don't know anything about sex for the sake of sex. I regret this, I am sure I have missed some bread and wine of life. I have known sex only as romantic love; and even when young I never questioned the charm of this attitude, any more than I questioned the facts of music or moonlight. I never considered categories of love as important, interesting, or confusing. And anyway the only thing to be said about romantic love is that it exists.

My first thoughts about love were like my first thoughts about beauty—that only a few people had it, that they could easily be recognized as love people. Then for years it didn't occur to me that there was anything in romantic love beyond the accolade of it; there didn't need to be, it was more than enough—unknown but complete.

I never talked with other children about what they thought. I was sure they had no thoughts that could compare with mine, I was sure that love was meant to be a mystery. And I never thought of children as having anything to do with it. I can't remember exactly what I did think of children—I saw lots of them about, and lots of parents, but since the latter never seemed to be in the category of love people I disregarded them.

86

I "played dolls," but the dolls never represented babies; they were just responsibilities for whom I built houses and put to bed at night before I could sleep. It never occurred to me to want one in life. Once I was given a large blue-eyed doll dressed as a baby, which embarrassed me. I asked a clever little girl I knew to make a lady's dress for her. More than anything else I loved to play paper dolls. I cut them out of magazines, made paper furniture for their houses which covered all the tables and commodes of a guest-room. All the other children I knew played with me. We each had a paper family, but while they concentrated on entertainments for their children I was interested only in my grown-ups. I had cut out the most attractive man I could find and a number of fatal women. He was called Sir Horace Grey and he had untold charm. There were children in his household but I could never feel that they belonged to him; I put them off to play by themselves where they would be happy. Sir Horace spent his life being in love, he could never get enough of it. His love monologues began in the morning and lasted through the day. The other children (the real ones) left their families and gathered around mine to follow the excitement. As I remember, Sir Horace never said much beyond "I am deliriously in love with you, you are so beautiful," but we all felt that something tremendous was always about to happen. Sir Horace continued his great words of love while all the children listened, holding their breath. Then I would build a paper carriage and Sir Horace and the latest lovely lady would get into it. They sat comfortably folded at the waistline and knees. He was always telling his plans and as my audience strained to hear I too would hear him say, "Now we will talk of love and drive deliriously through the spring woods."

I can't imagine anything more depressing than to have been born within the love pattern of those people in D. H. Lawrence or Hemingway books. It would be like spending the summer in town: iced drinks at intervals become the only things you look forward to, they take on a high sensuous value. I have no life in me that can be filled at this fountain. I have found romantic love where, alone, it can exist for me—in someone whose nature it is to regard sex as a mystery and a gift. Such people possess a formality of life, a prohibition against the direct, the undirected, the unstylized, the unlyrical, that make sex a rite rather than a function.

If anyone should ask me what I consider the right plans for romantic love—(no one ever asks me such questions but I spend much time making up answers)—I would say that they are based on three acknowledgments:

> Never consider it permanent. Consider
> only its permanent needs.
>
> Never expect it to equal your expectations.
>
> Never regard it as related to qualities,
> only to emanations.

I can think of any number of fatalities not to commit if you want to be wonderfully in love:

1. Never assume that the other person feels as romantic as you do.

2. Don't expect happiness—only rapture.

3. Don't be afraid of the tragic ending—romantic love is a tragedy to begin with.

4. Don't relate love to morals—chemistry is beyond morality.

5. Don't feel that you deserve more than you get—you'll get whatever your emanations call out, no more.

6. Romantic love is loss of identity. Behave with appropriate logic.

7. Don't think that what you *are* matters—it is only what you seem to be that counts.

8. Don't suffer out loud—even from behind closed doors it will repel.

9. Don't complain about anything—just leave the room, or the city, until you can act like an attractive stranger.

10. Don't fill the situation with *your* vibrations, you leave no room for the other person's.

11. Don't use endearments with rhythmic regularity.

12. Don't believe it's irresistible to state how much you're in love.

13. Don't exaggerate your emotions, they're already exaggerated.

14. Don't be dramatic, it's repulsive. Dramatize the other person.

15. Don't impose plans when the other person wants to read a book or take a nap or just enjoy the scenery.

16. Don't try to produce jealousy—this is an old and sick-making device.

17. Don't let it be sensed that you follow the other person with your eyes—it's maddening, unless his eyes are fixed on you.

18. Don't be naïve, it's infuriating; don't be skeptical, it's frightening.

19. Never be whimsical; *never* use baby talk.

20. Never mix love with duties, errands, telephone calls.

21. Never appear in completely new clothes after a separation—this can produce shock.

22. Never change your perfume.

23. Don't be mysterious, be private.

24. Don't be active when the other person wants a chance to act.

25. Don't be too fast or too slow, be tempered.

26. Don't ask questions that won't be answered; ask those which the other ego is waiting to answer.

27. Avoid sending the unsolicited photograph.

28. Don't hope to restrict the other person's personal efful-gence to yourself—it wouldn't be effulgence if it existed for you alone.

29. Remember that it is dangerous to remove your mask.

30. Remember that charm is more potent than intellect.

31. Remember that understanding is more potent than charm.

32. Always act as if it were Friday afternoon or Christmas Eve.

33. Try to arrange to live in meetings and partings forever.

Of course you never learn all these laws until you've lived a hundred years or so and have no further use for them. But if I am vain of my attitude toward love it is because, of those thirty-three suggestions, there are at least twenty-four which I have always obeyed instinctively, even before I knew what all the conflict was about. Therefore when I fell in love in the incurable romantic tradition I thought I would be more intelligent about it than anyone else. I was mistaken.

I was always trying to limit love to loveliness; and I was always trying to infuse it with ideas. Ideas had served me so well in so many realms that I was sure they would enhance romantic love. Once they did, but another time they didn't. That is the time I remember.

I was in love days, hours, minutes, for years. I don't think of it now as personal love, but rather as falling in love with an essence, a composite presence of those polarizations necessary for the state of romantic love. The circumstances of such love may be bright or dark, it doesn't matter—you stand within a magic circle unable to move. You are experiencing love-as-madness.

And now I scarcely know how to write of life within the circle. It has such power that you are blinded by it, you cannot remember it. Love-as-madness is meant to be felt, not remembered. When you are far from it, it becomes like a face which, through closed eyes, you try too hard to see; finally you cannot see it at all. I can think of this state, but I cannot *feel* it; to feel it you must be able to believe that such power resides within the sphere of a single presence

—but you cannot believe this unless you are experiencing it. You cannot feel night in the day or day in the night; the difference between knowing them and feeling them is too great—night and day must take place, not simply be remembered.

Perhaps other people escape the autocracies of the cerebral-sex type. I certainly don't see any of my friends in such plights. But then I don't see them in love either. It has been years since I have seen anyone who could even look as if he were in love. No one's face lights up any more except for political conversation. Did people used to look dazzled with love or did I just imagine they did? . . . But I remember someone describing Rupert Brooke when he was first in love . . . how it was almost unbearable to sit at the same table with him and the woman he loved—such was the incandescence of his face.

The world-well-lost was always the basis of romantic love to me. I tried never to let a day go by without turning it into a trance. I was so lost that I never knew where I was. I wasn't like a man without a country, I had too many countries and I was in all of them at once. Every country where I went, in love; every country where I had a telegram of love; every street or lane or path over which a postman came—all these places were, simultaneously, my home. I see myself in Tancarville, walking, blind with pain, losing my way, going into a garden where grapes were growing in the sun. I sat down among them, and then I was suddenly in Arles and Avignon, in Monte Carlo and Marly-le-Roi . . . I sat there until the sun went down, and then it occurred to me that I was nourished by my anguish, that I must produce a wish to be nourished otherwise or perish in a progression of waking dreams. Even my sleeping dreams reflected my floating life: I dreamed that I was playing the Lizst "Liebestraume" and wakened repeating the melody—sol mi-mi-mi, mi-mi-mi-*fa*—endlessly, not knowing what notes should follow after these.

The Art of Charm

Charm . . . a small cheap word or a great rich one. As for a definition . . . Animal magnetism?? Not to me. I love the snake-and-the-bird situation, but I never talk of the purely animal powers as charm. I notice that when I try to explain what charm means to me I always talk of pictorial or personality powers: the face I cannot help watching, the voice I wait to hear, the presence that is a glowing evidence of a special inner quality.

When I try to formulate the *kind* of inner quality, I mean the kind that implies a statement, offers an assurance. The statement: the purveyor of charm seems to be saying "Count on my imaginative understanding, it will not fail you." The assurance: the power of life is so strong in the charmer that I know he can engulf me in its radiance. The first is a "soul" quality; the second emerges in look, manner, intensity of emotion, conviction of thought, unconscious use of power, conscious reliance on that power.

I know a baby four years old, with a voice whose rising inflections I wait for; whose eyes look down, then up, and become a softer blue as she achieves the inflection. Then her charm continues: she says something when she speaks—I am always so pleased to know that what she says will be, first, a recognition of what has just been said; next, a follow-up of the announced idea; and, next, a necessity to make her comment on the idea and to make it interesting. By some sure instinct her comment is never banal. I am expectant before these phenomena; I am rewarded when I know in advance they will take place and that I will be there to observe them. In other words, I am charmed.

When you have found both types of charm in someone, you don't want to lose a moment of the presence that bestows it. You feel as you do when sitting in a room that is beautiful; you look around, your eyes are so rested, so pleased, that you can gather your life together and make it expand. Why sit in an ugly room?

You are a certain kind of person in the presence of charm, you are quite another person outside its radiations. In France I am always conscious of being in a country where charm is operative, on all levels. In America I never feel this at all; I feel that a whole continent exists like a doughnut around a hole; that hole is: lack of charm. In France I say "How do you do?" quite differently from the way I say it in America. In this country I hear people saying "How do you do?" with self-consciousness, or with no consciousness that it might be said "charmingly," as in my adopted country. When I try to "feel charming" in America I don't succeed.

You can be nourished by charm—it is like a food of finer substance . . . I remember lighting a fire in the salon, in the rue Casimir Périer. I remember Georgette coming in to sit down before it and holding out her hands to its rays. I thought, "Fire is a recurrent miracle to her; her response to it is a radiance; there is nothing I wouldn't do to invite, and bask in, this radiance." You come to feel that you can't live outside such effulgence; you can't imagine what it would be like to live without it. And then you know. Nothing ever prepares you for death and the loss of a life-transforming charm. Time is no healer, whatever people say. You feel more, not less, the bleakness of the regions unlighted by the rays of a great charm. I have said that in Georgette's presence I felt I was always smiling. Now I am all right, I can even laugh—I find many many things amusing, I laugh a great deal. But I cannot smile.

The Art of Writing

When we were in Vernet-les-Bains, and benumbed by want of money, I decided that if we were to go on living I had better write a book—it might sell and keep us alive for another year. In 1930 I had written a first book, *My Thirty Years' War*, which had not only kept us alive but had allowed us to buy the Citroên. I had written it with a great deal of pleasure and a certain amount of work, but I had no real knowledge of why I had made a success of it.

I didn't get on well with my second effort. When I had finished a second draft of the first two chapters I sent them to Solita for criticism—Solita Solano, great friend and superlative editor. She sent her opinion by return post:

"These pages have no charm in them. Your first book was full of charm. The art of that book, which you deny, was that you so intrigued your reader in your wild and *charming* life that he never had time to smell propaganda. And anyway, the story of your propaganda fight in which the reader is the bystander is not at all the same thing. In these pages you throw rocks at him. You're asking him to receive something in a way that will infuriate him with you and not with your ideas. It was easy for your reader in *Thirty Years' War* because he was hearing how other people had to swallow your propaganda. A much funnier business. In this ms. you have the air of laying down laws. Lay them down without having the air. Try hinting—just write the facts and let the reader have some fun. You will be surprised some day at the potential performance of a reader if given a little scope by you. And for heaven's sake come down off your high horse. Meet the reader on foot, introduce your best self, shake hands, take his arm and stroll quietly until, as in life, you engage his rabid interest in you and your ideas.

"*Law 1*. Don't write the way you feel about anything. Your feeling will come out in what you think about it.

"*Law 2*. No *general* statement about anything *generally* known, and very few general statements about the unknown.

"*Law 3*. Don't write down one single adjective or adverb until you've worked for them. And never use an adverb if you can help it.

"*Law 4*. Make your verbs work for you. The strength of great writing lies in verbs."

At this point I had a letter from Jane Heap who had also been reading my manuscript:

"Before I make any comment may I ask why you, who have never in your life in any situation played any game according to rules, should suddenly try to write a book according to rules? Just write *your* book and then let us see if you have done yourself into it, in front of it, through it, until it becomes only a frame for you. Use your brain on the manner and let the rest (matter) be spontaneous, welling up breathlessly as you tell things in life. Or throw out all that and give us a preachment—propaganda, wrestling with angels, devils or fools. I don't think your mind so good—your good moments are when your mind and emotions meet in an ecstatic embrace out in space beyond reason. You know the two birds on Chinese plates—souls of dead lovers meeting above and beyond the weight of life. Your brain is good to give heart-sticking form to your head, but mind is another matter—too precious to use much of in this kind of book. Why trip you up before you are started? I mean on words and swooning. Can't we give you a restorative later? Let's hear what you have to say in this delirium.

"I don't want to say anything really but *write*. You won't anger the reader unless you put too much brain into your attacks. If you make wild statements that are biffs in the eye he will take them if he can laugh—as I laugh at some of your more technical explanations, i.e., 'I have no shoulder-blades.' As Orage once said of you,

'If Margaret could only be herself consciously, what power she could have. She could confuse the best minds in all places and have a rich life. But she mustn't be confused herself.'

"I know you can unroll a world-beater if you just put your unknown self into it. Go to it the way you drive a car. Don't let them dis- or en-courage you. Drive on as you intend."

I agreed. I was comforted, understanding this kind of talk far better than the other kind. Still, how do I drive a car? There is nothing vague about it. At first I thought I drove with my mind; then, with my solar plexus; but finally I realized that I drove with my spinal column. It took me much longer to drive well than I had expected. Before I discovered exactly what to do to put myself in the position of magnetizing the car, I drove as many good drivers do —without the slightest professionalism. To drive with form —that is, with dash, control, freedom, authority, style and security—I had to put myself into a working relation to certain laws. There is nothing new about these laws of rhythm, but there is always something new in every person's adjustment to them.

I know precisely how I adjusted. First I adjusted the driver's seat so that I sat at a certain distance from the wheel, and at a certain distance above it, with the clutch and accelerator far enough forward to allow me to manipulate them without throwing my body off balance—as one sits on a high seat to drive a spirited horse, with one's feet braced against the dashboard. I sat firmly, in this upright position, with my spine at the waistline so placed against the chair back that it never need change position. All movements with arms flow from this fixed spine base; just as when sitting before a typewriter, or at a piano, scope of movement comes from the unmoving but relaxed spine. There are many ways of sitting before a typewriter but only one, for me, that allows hours of writing with rhythm and without fatigue. This depends wholly on the spinal pivot and I have a sensation that at its center of gravity there is one spot from which balance is produced—like the drop of water in a leveling-machine (I don't know what it's called). When you have found this equilibrium you feel that your torso and shoulders are poised lightly above the situation, able to pole-vault in any direction. The lightness comes from the fact that a perfect sitting-position enables you to breathe perfectly. Anyone can prove this, can change his driving by changing his breathing. If you fill your lungs with air before beginning to walk you have the sensation of being very light on your feet, completely in control of your movements, and your torso feels important —as if it contained a presence. If you want to walk along the street with anything like the satisfaction a panther must feel in prowling, you have to find one spot in your spine which will serve as axis; all your movement, which will become legato, will revolve about this axis.

If I wanted to write a book as I drive a car I should have to find that fixed point about which my life-movement had revolved. I began to suspect what it was.

Using this idea as a basis, I spent the beautiful sad autumn days in Vernet writing my book. I loved working at a *métier* about which I knew nothing—this forced me to create a *métier* of my own. But it was only in the morning that I had ideas and that words to express them came to me. I worked long and patiently to produce on paper the over-tones, only, of these ideas. To express them outright was fatal for some reason, my words became either feathers or stones. I learned that the best way for me was to keep one or two subjects firmly in mind and nearly always to write of something else.

This formula met with success. Solita wrote her approval: "Very good, and the tempo suits you. And you can offset it—the speed—by making at intervals an inter-mission—either of mood, or humor, or reflection or description. I don't mean a Chorus as much as I mean a balance—a compass—a comment that will point, charm, amuse. Like paprika—or a cocktail—or a sock in the emotional jaw. Or a pass of the hands—hypnotism. Each time different, but always the same stabbing reaction—or knuckles. Make it harder, make it softer, use art and skill —I should say, *métier*. Should say knowledge of cause and effect, awareness, judgment. Newsreel with breathing-spaces for thought (without comment)—moods—adorabil-ities—nervosities—charm—conversations—reflexions—a fear—a mania—a story—a memory. You have the entire world-psyche gamut. All is there for your use, like a piano."

... That phrase, "like a piano," took me back to Orage's words in 1924: "Remember you're a pianist, not a piano." It made me remember how I had always been the instrument that was acted upon, instead of the acting instrument. And it confirmed my suspicion as to that fixed point about which my life movement had revolved. I knew now exactly what it was, as exactly as I knew how I drove a car. I could name it in one word. The word was: self-love.

This revelation came to me slowly and it forms the next part of my book.

A LIFE FOR A LIFE

My third story, a box within the other two boxes, is about the event that changed us from one kind of people to another kind.

We had been preparing for this event even before we went to France. We expected it as the sequence of a search, and we had some intimation of the effect it might have upon our lives. But we didn't know that it was going to reorganize our "destinies." We didn't perceive this for a long, long time.

The first perceptible change we noticed in ourselves was that the subject-matter to which we had been most devoted began to interest us less. Art now had to take second place.

The time I am writing of is 1924. *The Little Review,* then ten years old, was still fulfilling its function as "the art magazine read by those who write the others." But this function no longer satisfied my conception of what a magazine should be. My dissatisfaction coincided with the new experience we were just beginning. As I look back at what now happened to me, I see that this experience was as inevitable as the one which made me start the *Little Review* in the first place. And now it wasn't the *Little Review* that mattered; and it wasn't Art that mattered any longer. It was Art's *raison d'être*.

The *Little Review* had created a legend (which many magazines of literature never do) because it wasn't merely a magazine of literature. Its material was an argument—life-or-death material. I didn't know this in 1914; I thought of the *Little Review* as a crusade which would prove the superiority of the artist mind over the intellectual mind. I didn't consider intellectuals intelligent, I never liked them or their thoughts about life. I defined them as people who care nothing for argument, who are interested only in information; or as people who have a preference for learning things rather than experiencing them. They have opinions but no point of view. They are "so articulate that you wonder if their words reflect their thoughts." Their talk is the gloomiest type of human discourse I know—the dullness of the *salon*, the talent of Mme. de Sévigné. This is a red flag to my nature. Intellectuals, to me, have no natures; they are like dinner parties where everyone exhibits information drawn from every source except himself. Such people will go anywhere to hear a new piece of music performed, whether they expect to be moved by it or not. They turn on their radios to hear new programs; I search the programs for well-known and too-well-loved music. I am indifferent to acquisition, I value experience—a receiving-station. This is the gulf between intellectuals and me—the reason why

they consider my type dilettante and amateur, why my
type considers them dilettante and amateur. (Or connoisseur, for all that it matters.) Intellectuals, I always felt,
might be bright but they weren't properly intelligent.
"Intelligent" to me meant to be right rather than wrong.
"Right" meant to be concerned about the nature of the
universe.

My first thoughts about the universe, and man's place and
function in it, trace back to an American Sunday-school.
It was presided over by my aunt whom I loved. I called
her Nantie and it was she who explained the sounds of
night to me and understood why I must keep getting out
of bed to see whether my dolls were sleeping before I
could sleep. She was very important in her religious authority and she really believed that the world had been
created in six days. From the beginning this had been
argued between us. I was only seven or eight but I had
already begun to argue; she was patient with this failing
because she had an ambition for me—I was to become an
Aimée MacPherson. On week days I was allowed to play
with her temple blocks and the twelve disciples made out
of cardboard. They were about six inches high, they stood
on little supports of wood and were painted on both sides,
so that you could turn them about without loss of illusion.
I remember that John the beloved was blue, Thomas
green, Judas red. But what excited me even more than
the apostles and their story was the creation story. To
illustrate this Nantie had made a series of charts—large
circles containing colored pictures of the elements created

by a personal God on each of the six days. All week I tried to argue her out of this fallacy and when Sunday came I went to Sunday-school early and sat in the front row where I could stare at her unpleasantly, daring her to tell the class this untruth. She always dared and no one ever objected.

I was so troubled by this situation that I think I never quite got over it. As I grew up and heard people talking about Darwin and evolution I experienced a great relief. But it was temporary. A few years later I remember an argument with the family doctor in which I stated that evolution was all right but it didn't explain everything —men didn't come from monkeys. I was apparently aligning myself with the position of man-as-another-formula, and this appears to have been my first stand for a conscious universe.

Years passed in which I remember no development of this theory. My only feeling of relation to a conscious universe was my consciousness of personal privilege—I always seemed to get what I wanted. My abstract distress had quieted into a periodic brooding—purely nostalgic— over the questions: What is the mystery of the universe? and what is the meaning of God? But I remember one day in college when an emotional minister made a speech in chapel, urging us to think of the meaning of life. At the end he asked those who wanted a higher life to stand up. I stood. When I saw that I was the only one of our law-breaking group on her feet I held my head higher and stood more firmly. The group jeered me afterward—I the leading lawbreaker standing up for an evangelist's pleadings. I was rather ashamed of having been so emotionalized, so I asked them defiantly what else anyone *could* want.

Then came years when I was sure I knew what everyone *should* want, since I had found it. Instead of earth, water, air and fire, the four elements of my personal universe had clearly emerged as music, love, nature and ideas. Of these religions the last led me almost to madness, certainly to many acts of the gravest fanaticism. I have broken off friendships because people didn't agree with my ideas; or I have argued with them until they broke with me, knowing that I would argue for the rest of our lives. It was this passion which made me start the *Little Review*.

In its early days people used to tell me that I had no critical sense, that I didn't know one thing from another. I always answered: I know the difference between life and death—in everything. This is all I wanted to know, this gave me my superabundance of superiority. We, the superiors, made experience out of nothing, we made life out of ourselves. We never found so much excitement outside as inside, we didn't travel because strange lands weren't as fascinating to us as ourselves. We could buy photographs of the Taj Mahal, but we couldn't recapture the conversations we might fail to have if we spent our time hurrying off to see such monuments. We were the people who knew things without learning them; we were the producers, rather than the product, of experience; our environment didn't condition us, we moulded our environment; enthusiasm was our validity, we knew

107

nothing about throwing cold water—except on the mediocre; bourgeois-ism went down before us as in a strong wind; we threw out the uninteresting and raised the interesting to incandescence; we didn't pass through thought to arrive at opinion, we leapt to resplendent conclusions; words were too slow for us, we traveled by e-motion. To me our superiority was so undisputed that I was over forty before I found anything that could challenge it.

My most intense days in this personal calendar were lived in California. Jane Heap had joined the *Little Review* and we were publishing it from a ranch house near Muir Woods, across the bay from San Francisco. We brought out a number made up of sixty-four blank pages, announcing that we had found no art to publish, that we hoped to find some for the next number.

We had never thought of art simply as painting, poetry, music, sculpture. We thought art was an expression, through the arts, of a need of something else. It was about this something else that we talked all those summer days. I remember the eucalyptus trees in the sun, the path beside them where we began to talk in the morning, walking up and down from the house to the barn. We walked up and down all day. When the sun set I used to feel that the day had been perceived by us alone on earth, for surely no other people had spent all of it, as we had, in wondering about the world.

From California we moved with the *Little Review* to New York. In summer we had a small grey house in Brookhaven, Long Island, where questions and answers went on forever. Under the blue locust trees, in shadows of sun and mist, we continued our shadowy speculations.

During this time we had read a book by Claude Bragdon which announced a coming book by a man named
Ouspensky. It appeared, under the title of *Tertium
Organum,* and we considered that we had found a con-
temporary author with a great mind. But what interested
us most about Ouspensky was the rumor that he was as-
sociated with a greater man called Gurdjieff. Ouspensky
was supposed to be writing a book about this man and
his ideas which would be called *The Unknown Doctrine.*

Alfred Richard Orage, former editor of the *New
Age* in London, came to New York as the percursor of
this doctrine. He had just spent two years in France study-
ing with the great man—so the story went—and if New
York showed any interest in the doctrine the legendary
Gurdjieff himself might come.

We went to the small theatre where Orage was to
talk with a feeling that our lives had waited always for
what might be said there. Everyone we knew was in the
audience—artists, intellectuals, socialites. We sat rather
far back, I remember, because we wanted to watch the
reactions of the audience. Mrs. Philip Lydig and Dr.
Percy Stickney Grant sat just in front of us, Claude Bragdon across the aisle.

Orage walked out upon the stage. He was tall and
easy, but quick and sure—the most persuasive man I have
ever known. He sat down and began to tell, simply, why
he had come. Claude Bragdon interrupted by standing up
to say that he had a letter from Ouspensky which he would
like to read. It was a conventional letter, everyone was

bored, Bragdon was unaware of boredom as he began commenting on the letter. Orage stopped him expertly and went on with his talk. But the ease and flow of the evening had been broken. "Talk louder," someone called out. "And be more interesting," Mrs. Lydig said loudly. This made me angry. "Don't do that," I whispered to her.— "What's the matter?" she said, still loudly, "don't you agree?"—"Of course not," I said, "just wait, he'll be so interesting he'll be incomprehensible." But he wasn't. He had no intention of being merely "interesting."

We went with Orage afterward, to a Child's restaurant, and asked him all the questions we had been hoarding. By midnight we had learned that this doctrine would not fulfill our hopes, it would exceed them.

And then Gurdjieff himself came.

It was announced that the Gurdjieff group would give its special "dances" in the Neighborhood Playhouse, and all New York gathered again. Orage read explanatory notes for each dance, and everyone in the audience (except the genus intellectual) realized that he was in the presence of a manifestation which had its roots in a source of which we know nothing. Our sense of this phenomenon was so sharp that we almost forgot about the man Gurdjieff, who was supposed to be somewhere behind the scenes directing the dances. From my seat down front I saw him for a moment in the wings, commanding his pupils, exhorting them to greater, and ever greater, precision. When we went back later to find Orage I had just time to look carefully at a dark man with an oriental face, whose life

seemed to reside in his eyes. He had a presence impossible
to describe because I had never encountered another with
which to compare it. In other words, as one would immediately recognize Einstein as a "great man," we immediately recognized Gurdjieff as the kind of man we had never
seen—a seer, a prophet, a messiah? We had been prepared from the first to regard him as a man different
from other men, in the sense that he possessed what was
called "higher knowledge," or "permanent knowledge."
He was known as a great teacher and the knowledge he had
to offer was that which, in occult books and in the schools
of the East, is given through allegory, dialogue, parable,
oracle, scripture, or direct esoteric teaching. From what
Orage had told us we knew that Gurdjieff presented his
knowledge in a terminology which would not alienate the
factual minds of Western thinkers. We had never been
ranged among the factual; but neither had we ever been,
nor could we ever be, satisfied with the purely mystical
or metaphysical.

We looked upon this man standing in the wings of
the Neighborhood Playhouse in New York City as a
messenger between two worlds, a man who could clarify
for us a world we had hoped to fathom—the world which
the natural scientists had revealed but not interpreted.

I think I really thought of Gurdjieff, at first, as a
sort of Hermes, teaching his son Tat. But while it was
impossible to understand the Hermetic dialogue, merely
by reading it or speculating about it, I felt that the essence
of the Emerald Tablet itself might be made understand-
able to us through Gurdjieff's method of teaching. What I

111

mean exactly is this: that what philosophers have taught as "wisdom," what scholars have taught in texts and tracts, what mystics have taught through ecstatic revelation, Gurdjieff would teach as a science—an exact science of man and human behavior—a supreme science of God, world, man—based on sources outside the scope, reach, knowledge or conception of modern scientists and psychologists.

Later, at Carnegie Hall, another series of dances was given. Plans had been made for an accompaniment of four pianos but as it turned out there was only one, played by M. de Hartmann with the percussive splendor demanded by Gurdjieff. These dances were taken from, or based upon, sacred temple dances which Gurdjieff had seen in the monasteries of Tibet, and their mathematics were said to contain exact esoteric knowledge. New York was still interested, but the intellectuals had begun to complain that the performers' faces didn't register "joy" as they danced. I suppose these critics would have been pleased by an Isadora Duncan expressiveness over the movements of the planets in space.

We spent all the time we could with Orage, listening to the ideas of Gurdjieff. And then one night Gurdjieff himself talked. He presented his ideas as not new but as facts always known and always hidden—that is, never written down but passed from age to age through the teachings of the great initiates. "Initiate" had always been a word that left us cold, if not hotly antagonized, because of the nebulous thinking of the people who used it. But now we had no time to waste in revolt over words. The substance of Gurdjieff's doctrine was, for all of us, for the first time, an answer to questions.

All our lives our questions had been, we thought, everyman's questions; but everyman seemed satisfied with answers which didn't satisfy us. If a great scientist said, "We can erect a coherent system dealing with all aspects of human knowledge and behavior by the refinement, extension and continued application of the methods which have been so successful in the exact sciences," we said, "No, you can't, there's something you won't be able to get at with those methods." If a great doctor said, "Prayer is power," we said, "Yes, it must be, but why?" If a great philosopher based his doctrine on the "incalculable forces of the spirit," we knew what he was talking about, but the phrase was vague. What *are* those forces? What more, if anything, can be learned about them? We found more meat* in Hermes: "For the Lord appeareth through the whole world. Thou mayest see the intelligence, and take it in thy hands, and contemplate the image of God. But if that which is in thee be not known or apparent to thee, how shall He in thee be seen, and appear unto thee by the eyes? But if thou wilt see Him, consider and understand the sun, consider the course of the moon, consider the order of the stars."

But since astronomers had no revelations to make (except physical ones), and since no philosopher had ever spoken clearly about what it is to "know thyself," we were left stranded. All we could do was to reiterate: in that

*"Substance," I think today, is a better word.   *113*

region between physics and philosophy is there no firm ground for the mind's construction of a faith?

Gurdjieff's statement was that there does exist a super-knowledge, a super-science; and what he had to say about it convinced us that we would never hear anything else to compare with it, never find anything else which could illuminate the great texts to which we had always wanted to give a reverent investigation.

When he spoke of the "way" in which this knowledge could be acquired—a way which brought you gradually into a "condition of knowledge"—we were ready to believe that it might indeed be a way for us. But though we suspected the magnitude of the knowledge, we didn't realize how different its development and application would appear to us fifteen years after our first encounter with it. And we certainly hadn't the faintest idea how difficult this particular "way" would sometimes be.

After his appearance in New York Gurdjieff left for France where, in Fontainebleau-Avon, he had established his "Institute for the Harmonious Development of Man." People from all parts of the world, to whom his cosmology had become a way of life, were living and working in the Institute. Orage and the group that had come to New York were returning with Gurdjieff.

And so it was that in June, 1924, Georgette, Jane, Monique and I—as well as several other people who felt as we did—left New York for Paris. We knew the import of our decision: we had prepared to "cast aside our nets" and follow.

MARGARET ANDERSON
photograph by Berenice Abbott

MARGARET ANDERSON
portrait by Pavel Tchelitchew
(collection of Mr. & Mrs. Zachary Scott)

the Author at the Château de Tancarville

the Author at Hendaye, about 1940

GEORGETTE LEBLANC
at the Château de la Muette

GEORGETTE LEBLANC
in the salon at the Château de la Muette

the Château de Tancarville

the Château de la Muette

2. It was late when we arrived at Cherbourg and the train for Paris left at midnight. I didn't like traveling through the night, I liked to watch the French countryside by day and drink my *vin rosé* looking out the *wagon restaurant* at a new French spring.

Though we couldn't afford it, we went to our favorite hotel—the old Beaujolais on the Palais Royal Gardens. Our rooms were numbers 14, 15 and 16—two of them as long and narrow as railroad coaches, and each with a bathroom in a partitioned corner. These narrow chambers with their beautiful *boisseries* had once been palatial and their windows framed the great perspective of arcades and ancient houses, one of which was Cardinal Richelieu's. Monique and I went to the Conciergerie and bought white flowers to vivify our wine-red walls.

All day in the royal gardens birds sang, children sailed boats in the fountain and played under the clipped trees; French clerks and *la petite bourgeoisie* walked about without aim, sat on the benches and watched the children; in the afternoon chess players gathered in the rotonde (since removed) and thought for hours in clouds of smoke; at seven o'clock a guard locked the garden gates, lighted the old street lamps, and sometimes a night wanderer strolled softly under the galleries.

But we couldn't linger on in this stage-set, it cost money. All we needed was a *pied-à-terre* from which we could go back and forth to Fontainebleau, and my choice fixed itself upon the family house in Passy which was being closed for the summer. I decided that we must be in

115

it, whatever the strain. We opened negotiations which ended in success—of a kind. To make sure of our gratitude the family announced that they had had a chance to rent the house for twenty thousand francs—though they knew that we knew that this was a fabrication. When we moved in we found that the principal rooms had been closed. But it didn't matter. We sat late that night in the Peter Ibbetson garden and talked of our future. The next morning we went to the Gare de Lyon and bought tickets for Fontainebleau.

3. *Fontainebleau-Avon.* From the station we walked down the road to Avon, to the end of the village where a forest begins. At the right was a garden door in a high wall. Jane pulled the bell and it tinkled long and softly. A boy with alert eyes opened the door, smiled without curiosity, and asked us to come in. He said that Mr. Gurdjieff had driven to Paris, would be back for dinner; would we walk through the gardens where we would find our American friends.

We entered a grass courtyard enclosed by the château and the wall. It had the aspect most becoming to courtyards—that of a garden half-abandoned. In the center was a fountain; its gentle water dropped upon stone night and day. The boy led us through the château, which had once belonged to Mme. de Maintenon and was now called the Château du Prieuré. It was not wide but long, its salons opened both upon the entrance court and the formal gardens in front. Beyond were forests which led over pine-lined roads to the village of Moret, on a lovely river with the unlovely name of Loing.

We stood for a long time on the terrace, among urns and balustrades and all the brighter flowers, drinking in once more the divine light and air of France. The gardens were long, a fountain sprayed their stillness, and beyond them were stone benches under an arbor of yew trees (perhaps not yew, but I always felt they were). The kitchen gardens were far in the distance and we found our friends there among the vegetables.

They took us through the château and indicated vacant rooms we were to choose from. The principal bedrooms were over the salons and some American had named this wing the Ritz. It was used for transient guests. Two other floors, with small bedrooms, were called the Monastery. We chose our cells here, mine over the diningroom garden, Georgette's toward the forest. Jane chose a room at the back that looked into a farmyard, because she liked to be wakened by crowing cocks. Here there was a small stable that had already become a legend because Katherine Mansfield, during her last illness, had lain in the loft, breathing the healthy smell of cows and hay.

At dinner there were perhaps twenty people at the table; others, responsible for the feast, ate nearer the kitchens. We were surprised to see Ouspensky among the guests, having heard that he had left the Institute for good. On this first night we were curious about Ouspensky. He sat at Gurdjieff's left and acted like a small boy, laughing more than he meant to, saying what he meant not to, flushing with the armagnac forced upon him. This situation wasn't to Ouspensky's detriment, it is the lot of everyone who passes through the Gurdjieff life-class. As we learned later, the ritual of toasts, in armagnac, had to do with the psychology of human types. And since important matters were never explained to you in this school until you yourself came upon them—through long experience and repetition *ad nauseam*—it took me many years to understand the hierarchy of the toasts, or to apply it to myself and others with even the beginning of accuracy. Though Ouspensky must have taken part in this ceremony a hundred times, I always felt that he had never discovered its significance; that he knew ideas but didn't know people. Gurdjieff's doctrine of the "unknown" began with man the unknown.

The doctrine was embodied in an enormous manuscript on which Gurdjieff was working day and night.

During our first months at the Prieuré, Gurdjieff was personally inaccessible—at least to our group. We saw him at meal-time, in the study-house after dinner during the dances, in the salon for readings of the manuscript, at café tables in Fontainebleau for the translation of new chapters, sometimes in his car for trips which most people hoped to avoid, as they were nerve-racking. But he wasn't available for personal communication or instruction. He had finished one phase of teaching and had not yet begun upon the next.

Even now I cannot attempt to describe Gurdjieff. I would feel as if I had been asked to write a description of Nature in all her moods. And I cannot talk of the

118

material of his teaching, of its method or its meaning. I can tell what it did to me, that is all. It is adjusted differently to every individual, and everyone would tell of it differently. It is completely different from what I imagined it would be, from what I understood it to be, stage by stage. It is not a story of learning something through the mind, or of assimilating something that is told to you. It is a story of a new education, of taking whatever degree your heredity and upbringing, your wish and your will, make possible. It has no relation to psychoanalysis or any of the other modern introspections. Introspections into what? into what non-existence? It is a cleansing and a filling. Its science consists in the precision with which you are charted, by which you are aided—slowly enough not to break you, fast enough to keep you in that state of wonder, surprise, shock, torment, remorse, reward, which alone taps your potential forces. The first statement I heard Gurdjieff make about his teaching was: "I cannot develop you; I can create conditions in which you can develop yourself."

The Institute had been in operation for two or three years before we arrived and I remember the people who were working there as some of the most interesting people I have ever known. One especially, from Constantinople, became a great friend of ours. In her outer manifestations she personified what they had all tried to attain— a holding-in rather than a going-out. She was a genial kind of person but she always made you conscious of a silence in her. She didn't tell you what she "thought" about anything. At first this puzzled and exasperated me; I still

measured people by expressiveness and thought by expression. I decided that she didn't think, or that she was in-
articulate. Later I noticed that she talked rather vaguely
of anything at all until she was questioned. Then she
answered with economy, holding herself to the frame of
your question, offering no more than it called for. After
a few weeks of this technique I came to feel a power in
it. This woman didn't thrust herself at you, it was as if
she realized that one has very little self to thrust. She
gave you no stories of her inner life, she seemed to know
that no one has any inner life worth mentioning. Of course
there were other people in the group who had mastered
few or none of the realities that were being taught. They
were as vain as people everywhere in life who express
their "personalities" at all times.

Orage was at the Prieuré when we arrived. He and
his wife, with several other pupils from New York who
had been there before, formed our immediate group; but
there were also new people from France, England, Germany and points east. According to type, each got something, nothing, or everything out of being there. Everyone
who came knew the fantastic stories of the Institute's purpose which had been imagined and reported—from Katherine Mansfield's vague spiritual interpretations to the
definitely gross ideas of certain Frenchmen or the naïve
generalizations of certain Americans.

One of our New York friends, a *Little Review* con-
tributor, stayed at the Prieuré only one day. She asked
intellectual questions and received allegorical answers.
She began to feel spiteful. "If there's anything in all this,"

she said, "someone can put it into a phrase for me. Otherwise I won't know whether I'm for it or not." None of the Gurdjieff people tried to put anything into a phrase, though Jane did her best by saying, "It's a method to keep your past from becoming your future." Our New York friend ignored this. "I don't know why they won't talk," she said, "I asked the least anyone can ask." No one disputed this and she left the next day. Fourteen years passed before I saw her again, when she came into Michaud's to dine one night and sat at our table for coffee. I didn't know what she thought about anything at this time, but when she thought of us she evidently thought of religion because she said, "Still learning to be good?" I didn't know what to answer, I could think of no phrase that would catch her attention. Instead of speaking I sat and thought about her, and fourteen years, and observed the sadness of life. It wasn't that she looked older, her face was unlined and her vitality unworn. But fourteen years of the same reflexes, mannerisms, reactions, gestures, postures, expressions, had traced their paths on her psyche as associations plough through the grey of the brain. I knew in advance exactly what she would say, having heard it in the years before, so I didn't listen; instead I watched her mannerisms announce in advance what she would say. This pantomime, unconscious and sculptural, composed a tragedy. When a line formed at the corner of her mouth and drew it down in a bitterness deeper than ever before, I knew that she was going to say, "Well, that's the way it is." It was like watching an actor walk upon a stage in the rôle of Vanity, giving a photographic performance

121

of the visible signs of self-love upon the organism. But what impressed me most was the length of time that passed between the beginning and the end of the mouth's gesture and the beginning of the spoken phrase. It hadn't been so long, years ago; now it seemed a full minute. I thought of someone's definition of Gurdjieff's teaching as a "method of acceleration." I thought of all the kinds of acceleration I had watched since my first contacts with people who had accelerated.

Of all the people who came to the Prieuré while I was there, no one was ever asked to stay if he wanted to leave, and no one was asked to leave if he really wished to stay. Some were not received at all. One well-known woman*came out from Paris expecting to be received as a celebrity. Gurdjieff didn't know who she was but he saw her from a window when she arrived. She was told he wasn't there. The story of his brief explanation of course went the rounds—at least to the three of us who always had our ears at the psychological keyhole: her vanity was too fixed, it would take years to break it up; she was not young, the chances were against success, his effort would be disproportionate since hers would probably be non-existent.**

Another quick flight was made by an American woman who stayed only three days. She reacted to new situations as if they were old ones. This made her angry and she left in disdain. One of the most touching people who fled was the man who said he hadn't the courage to start on what might be only another wild-goose chase after knowledge. He left sadly. There was an Englishwoman

122

* Gertrude Stein.

** He did receive her once, later.

who identified everything she heard with her own idea
of Buddha, and then left to continue a life devoted to her
own nebulous conception of "know thyself"; and there
was another woman who announced that you could find
a hundred such teachers in the world, that this doctrine
was no more interesting than any other. If we hadn't
already heard enough to know its uniqueness (at least for
our time and place in the world) we might have been influenced by all the cross-currents—the people who called
it and us too material, those who said we were hypnotized, those who predicted our decline into mysticism or a
sort of super-metaphysics. But it would have taken a lot
of effort to be influenced by people who discovered only
mysticism in the most lucid formulations, and who sensed
neither mystery nor knowledge in the most paradoxical.
So we simply got to work on the doctrine, and on ourselves. And there was nothing simple about either activity.

Outwardly, at the Prieuré, we felt that our days were
numbered. Inwardly we felt that we had been given a key
to a new model of the universe.

Outwardly we didn't go through any of the training
that the older pupils had demonstrated in New York.
That was over for the moment, Gurdjieff was finishing the
last chapters of his book, and everyone was absorbed in
translation from Russian into English, French, German.
Besides this we worked in the kitchen gardens, we
straightened garden paths ("Too slow," Gurdjieff said,
walking by, "must find way to do in half time.") We
cut grass and helped to cut down trees. I had a small silent

123

portable piano which I sometimes took out under the yew trees to practise on. "Waste of time," Gurdjieff said, walking by with the musician, M. de Hartmann; "must find shortcut." I sought out the musician later, hoping for interpretation. He began: "Arensky had only four fingers on one hand but he could play anything and play it as he wanted to. Question of engineering." Then he gave me so much new information about techniques and the mechanics of bodies in relation to instruments that I was tempted to return to Art.

But I had not gone to Gurdjieff to learn more about Art; I wanted to learn more about the universe. If anyone had asked me exactly what I wanted to find out, and if I could have answered as simply as a child, I would have said, "I want to know what is God." When I realize now how I might have related this wish to an essential conduct, and how I couldn't, I am appalled. If I had known how to ask a question, if I could have been simple (I who have always been so sure of simplicity), I could have asked, "What does it mean—'in My Father's house there are many mansions'? What does it really mean?" Or "Will you tell me something about the Last Supper?—why does religion seem to offer no real interpretation of this sacrament?" I wouldn't have received answers that could be regarded as answers, since "what" and "why" were always discouraged at the Prieuré and only "how" was sometimes rewarded; but I might have started ten years earlier on that break-up of my own image which precedes any *study* of man created in the image of God. As it was, "God" was not mentioned in this place after the day when someone at the table succeeded in a direct question and Gurdjieff answered "You go too high." I never found a way to overleap these barriers, made for leaping. I had so much awe of all that I heard, I was so convinced that I would learn what it meant through some extension of the mind, that I could think only of studying it, discussing it with everyone—that is, continuing to live as I had always lived, by imagining what I could of the ideas involved, hoping that everyone else's imagination would work too, and believing that if we thought and discussed long enough we would come upon revelation.

I don't regret the endless discussions—these first years of the Gurdjieff abstractions were a golden age to me. But if you linger on in it you never arrive at essentials. When you get beyond it you realize why all the stories told about Gurdjieff's presentation of the Hermetic wisdom are surface stories. I have yet to see in print, even in the two respectable articles written by men who have worked with him, a single indication of the concrete substance of his mentation. Someone writing anonymously said: "For me the most sensational aspect of Gurdjieff's work was a sort of sublime common sense. I mean that my experience resembled many times those of the initiate in antiquity who was asked by his friends how he felt when he was told the secrets of an occult brotherhood. 'Like a fool,' he said, 'for not having seen for myself the truths they taught.'" After my golden age I never felt this facility of seeing-for-one's-self. "You don't mean that there's anything really secret about this doctrine, do you?" people have asked me for years. How answer such a question? In two ways perhaps. Either there are no secrets, or— nothing but secrets. Atoms aren't as secret as they were, someone has charted them and broken them up.

But in 1925 atoms hadn't been bombarded and broken and neither had I. The Prieuré of my day was not the Institute where pupils were wakened at all hours, pushed beyond their second-wind into real fatigue, their life-habits turned into too-difficult new patterns. All this came to me later, in quite another form. The Prieuré I remember is a place where reverent study filled the days and nights. After dinner we went to the study-house— originally an airplane hangar from war days, later converted by Gurdjieff into a place for work. The floors were covered with oriental rugs and we sat on cushions arranged in two tiers around the walls. There was a large low stage on which pupils worked out the intricate sacred dances. Usually Gurdjieff began the evening at the piano, composing the music for a new dance-movement which M. de Hartmann scored simultaneously; then the pupils began to work it out under Gurdjieff's instructions, always given in a mental shorthand that sounded far too rapid to be understood. But the woman from Constantinople and several others translated the commands into movement almost as swiftly as M. de Hartmann had made the piano orchestration. Sometimes afterward, if there were guests who wanted to understand the aim of the Institute, Gurdjieff would talk. This talk was always geared to three audiences— the guests, the pupils, and Gurdjieff himself; that is, first, what the guests would make of it; what the pupils would

learn of the guests and of themselves as they listened to
Gurdjieff; and what Gurdjieff himself would learn of the
guests and the pupils.

Afterward we would go to our rooms and "philoso-
phize" over what we had heard. The subject-matter that so
engrossed us was not material we had heard before,
though we might have discovered it in Hermes, Buddha,
the Bible, had we known how to. Gurdjieff's terminology
was completely new; but what held our attention and
stretched our minds was the body of knowledge to which
the terminology was applied: a study of man's psyche
from the standpoint of an exact science, illuminating the
mystery of the processes by which a man can be said to
be born again.

"Unless a man be born again . . ."—this was the
keynote of Gurdjieff's science, his work, his effort, his
example. For this reason he had no patience with the man
who merely "philosophizes"; his interest was in the man
who "can do." Later we were to understand a great
deal about this distinction.

I see now that we lived those first great years of
Gurdjieff's teaching in clouds of conviction that we were
not treating it as a philosophy. Because the ideas involved
in this science were new to us, we thought our reactions
to them were new. Because our minds were exploring
this knowledge, we assumed that our hearts were understanding it. We thought we had already outgrown those
self-regarding inflations for which Gurdjieff had a one-
word description: "psychopathic." We thought we were already well advanced on the road to self-knowledge. How

far we still had to go even to make a start was, fortunately, hidden from all of us.

4. Life seems to be an experience in ascending and descending. You think you're beginning to live for a single aim—for self-development, or the discovery of cosmic truths—when all you're really doing is to move from place to place as if devoted primarily to real estate. Looking back I see myself *en voyage*, clutching my suitcase of Gurdjieff ideas, convinced that my only property lay inside it, but spending four-fifths of my time searching a home "where we could really work." In those brief intervals of home peace the real emphasis was on home rather than on cosmos. Of course we gave our minds to the latter and to the "terror of the situation" presented by our inertias; but since inertia is man's tradition, could we by our own efforts "push back civilization single-handed," as Orage so often said? We read and reread the Gurdjieff manuscript, but I began to feel that there must be something *to do* that we weren't doing. I still reacted to our meetings and discussions with exaltation, but I knew this state to be simply my capacity for being moved. Pushed to its extreme it becomes the mystic's ecstacy, anything can be believed in such a state. I was not made to be a mystic; I have always been skeptical of faith without science. The real object of this quest was surely that injunction about being born again. Were we approaching such a condition? I couldn't see that we were.

I didn't minimize the actual transvaluation of all values which seemed to me the most important by-product of our investigation—so important that I wanted to spend my time proselytizing for them. I thought people would take to great ideas as motors take to gasoline. But they didn't, they simply continued to say, "I'm all against this looking into one's self—it's dangerous." "Of course it may be dangerous," I said, "unless you keep on looking." I could never understand why they wouldn't face this danger as well as any other. Was it that what they saw in themselves frightened them more than other dangerous sights?

In trying to apply the Gurdjieff values to human behavior, our most passionate arguments always took place over art and religion—since you can't convince an artist that art isn't mankind's noblest expression, and you can't convince a religionist that there exists a more elevated conception of Good and Evil than the one he holds. I have lost years of youth trying to persuade religionists that Boehme was right when he said, "Anyone who hasn't learned that there is no more good (God) in one thing than in another is still a child."

I remember one all-night struggle with a religious group which Jane summed up like this: "You people are talking of an emotional experience—religion. You say we make a god of the mind because we are talking of something that is experience on three planes. Your emotional experience can be compared to a dog's joy in greeting his master. Because a dog has only two planes of experience. I'm not minimizing the dog's experience, but your statements reduce all humanity to animals."

I continued to believe that all this talk would make people stop, look and listen. "Why do you think so?" Jane said. "Look at your results." She was right, my results couldn't have been more disastrous if I had been advocating murder instead of self-development.

One day Orage asked me, "Why are you always arguing about right and wrong?"

"Because I'm going to convince people," I said.

"But you know you can't."

"No, I don't. I believe that if I can present these ideas intelligently enough ——"

"Good heavens," he said, "you don't really believe that people are ever convinced of anything by listening to ideas?"

"Of course I do," I said. "What other way is there?"

"There are only three ways of influencing people," he said—"magnetization, competition, example."

I was always running up against the injunction that "by taking thought a man cannot add a cubit to his stature." The Gurdjieff mentation was supposed to be the wedge that entered just here. "The brain is not an organ with which to arrive at truth. The brain is just a muscle. 'Mind' as we know it merely uses words, formulates reactions, runs out a chain of associations, repeats received ideas, stirs up a heap of impressions received passively." This statement led to a summation: "The first step in becoming an adult is to realize that things are done *to* us, not *by* us."

There, within a sentence, was a concept with dimensions. There, within the framework of the concept, was the quintessence of a theory and a technique which Gurdjieff presented not as a unique theory but as a unique activity. There, in a single formulation, was expressed our adherence to this unknown doctrine in which, for the first time, we were hearing things that were not merely repetitions of things we had already heard.

I was quite willing, I thought, to give up my loyalty to the mind. But I wanted to be convinced, or to convince myself, that I was approaching a process higher than taking thought. I believed that if the potentiality of such a faculty existed we would find it in this doctrine. But I didn't for a moment believe we had yet done so. When would we? Why hadn't we already? Because of some obstacle, unknown to us, within ourselves? I hadn't yet the vision to know whether this was so or not; and, if it was, of what the obstacle consisted.

Of course I knew that this knowledge runs through all great legends, allegories, parables; that it can be found in the whole scale from fairytales to scripture; that it is suggested in all great systems of thought, in all great schools—Hermes, the Gnostics, the Essene monks, Pythagoras . . . Of course, I kept saying to myself, we were digging out the findings and building up the parallels; we were learning why there is no real religion in the world, why the words of Jesus Christ have not been understood, why "God is not known or worshipped, merely used"; why most religious interpretation has been distortion; why true religion means something else; why the something else is never written down, never referred to except under the protection of formal thought; why it is never offered for nothing, why a life must be given to find this Life. We thought we were ready to give our lives for it. But how were we to discover, unaided, the unwritten demand behind the immense abstractions? Of course we were being aided by Gurdjieff, but the aid was offered in those terms which I had not yet come to understand: "I cannot develop you; I can create conditions in which you can develop yourselves." What was it that we were to *do*, beyond trying to "take impressions actively," so that things would be done by us, not to us? All the keys to this enigma were perhaps offered in the Gurdjieff manuscript but, as its author said, they were placed far from the locks.

I felt that all my speculation continued to be purely imaginative, and I knew that Orage had a definition of "imagination" which left you without any pride in this faculty. "Imagination as we use it," he said, "is simply an excess of desire over ability."

In our desperate and impersonal self-examination we would meet for discussion and try to illuminate ourselves about ourselves. To all of us Jane's formulations for self-questioning were the most vital. She would present questions like the following and we would try to dig out the answers:

1. How much of your life is an illusion (the world as it appears to you through the distortions of lack of self-knowledge)?
2. How many failures or negative results (from well-intentioned, well-conceived, hopeful plans) do you think were caused by your illusion being too patent to others—with other illusions? Have

you ever had a glimpse of the extent to which you rest under self-hypnosis? Have you ever been aware of the power of self-love as an hypnotic force?

3. Have you ever had a moment of realization of the spectacle of human beings going through life in a state of deep hypnosis?

4. Could you ever detach yourself enough from your illusory world to conceive a world of Reality—in which each person perceived Reality as one and the same thing—not interpreted by the whims, vanities, likes and dislikes of a reacting animal? but perceived by a permanent, understanding three-fold "I"—able to use the chemistry and vibrations of his type consciously instead of always being acted upon from the outside (as we are)?

We asked Orage: "Is contemplation the process higher than taking-thought?"

"No," he said. "Contemplation is the last note in the thinking octave, but only the first note in the octave of a higher process."

What interests me now, as I review our evolution in the Gurdjieff teaching, is that for so long I never doubted that all our talk and "thinking" would provide the desired self-development. Of course talk gives you almost as much new gland life as being in love does. But why, since I knew that being in love doesn't necessarily lead to anything beyond being in love, did I assume that talk inevitably leads to something beyond talk—for instance, to Being? It took me so long to find the right answer to this question that I have never since been able to look back upon my thinking past with pleasure.

5. During most of these middle years of our great experience Gurdjieff was not easily accessible. It may be that he would have been, if we had known how to need what he had to offer.

In the autumn of one of these years we had to face a fact that none of us knew how to face. Orage died. In England.

6. The year 1934 had come and we*were still in Vernet when we heard that Gurdjieff was in Paris. Then came the news that he was accepting a small group for special teaching.

From Paris I received reports of this teaching— daily pages of accurate transcription made by someone** going through the almost unbearable tension of dying to an old life. The effort to pass on this experience to me was a labor of love and I doubt that I, under the same circumstances, could have accomplished it for anyone, however much I might have wanted to.

As I reread these notes today I come upon a formulation in two words—a noun followed by a verb of such extensions that you feel you can never again regard any fact without examining it under the influence of this verb. Of course two words on a piece of paper are open to any interpretation that two thousand million people can give them. Everything, in the end, is interpretation. But *what* interpretation?

You can take three phrases like "A tooth for a tooth,

134 * Georgette and I.

    ** Solita Solano.

an eye for an eye, a life for a life" and interpret them in any way you like. But to knock out someone's tooth or pluck out someone's eye for your own lost tooth or eye, to kill someone because he has killed someone else—these retaliations can't be the meaning. No one ever gave me a hint, in my young days, that these three phrases present a picture, on three planes, of man's three interacting systems. We *do* have second teeth that replace baby teeth; we *do* develop an eye to see those things which are unseen; we *do* have to give up one kind of life to find another kind.

But no parents or teachers or religionists seem to know the under-meanings. They simply say, "The words of Jesus are clear and cannot be misunderstood by anyone who wants to understand them." Wants to—and then what?

Up to this point in my pilgrim's progress I had tried to build my thinking on the following model: "Think large true facts, seen as forms—such as the organization of the universe. Forms of thought are energies. Think: from birth to death we are immersed in actions, we fitfully guide ourselves away from or toward things; we cannot hold before our minds for one second the whole evidence about anything. The mind's object is to grasp the facts as wholes. Elevate yourselves. Seek out emotions and thoughts that are appropriate to a mind. That is self-feeding. Everything eats everything else—the universe feeds itself."

The statement that most fired my imagination, I remember, was this one: "After a certain rate of vibration everything in the universe becomes psychological. Air and light = psychological food. The transmutation of substances."

But what was I to do with this thought? I couldn't *think* beyond the fact that the visible physical world is the physical body of the universe. Then I must bring in "As above so below." All right, I too have a physical body— I can see it.

All right, then the next step must obviously be: "The human body is given you to understand the universe." All right. Next: "We are made up of, are replicas of, the universe." Well, if the human body "is made like an electric station, generating and wasting energy," it is here that that transmutation of substances comes in. Transmutation would lead to a very great thought: "the self-regeneration of man: an effort at reproduction—a succession of bodies in ourselves, each of a higher vibration." In other words, immortality? Well, all right. I certainly know that I have something more than a physical body. I have an emotional body and a mental body. But how, in thought, am I going to relate these bodies, which I can't see, to higher substances of the universe, which I can't see? No, thought comes to an end. Try images, then. All right: man made in the image of God. But I couldn't complete the image. Beyond thought and image I was waiting, waiting for that knowledge-to-come of As-Above-So-Below, which I felt would one day burst upon me in a blinding light. In a way it seemed so simple an image that no one could fail to construct it step by step. In another way it seemed that no

136

man would ever do it, that we would continue to exist only "in relation to a mystery."

November, December, January, February, March were still to come and Georgette and I were to spend them in Vernet, out of contact with the man in Paris who was helping a group of people step by step into the knowledge of that process higher than taking thought.

I was so tormented by our absence from this source that I began to dream of our predicament. I hadn't dreamed for years, but now I had a dream like an old mystery play. In it we were slaves, but at the same time we were actors in a drama, in which the rôles had been distributed for conscious playing. We walked as a pageant through life, yet we were walking on a stage. There were two columns at its ends, with wide steps between them leading away from the audience. We came on at the left, in a long procession, walking slowly. At the center of the stage we turned our backs to the audience and walked down the steps. When it came my turn I was too tired to go beyond the first step, I sat down on it to rest. The slaves behind me were held up, they tried to push me on, crying that I would be beaten if I stayed there. I said, "We are such tortured people, we can bear no more." Then I noticed that I was sitting with my hands on my knees, that I had raised my head and was looking straight out before me. In a flash there passed through me a vision, like those told by mystics, of ineffable impression, in which the meaning of all life appeared to my consciousness. I thought: I may never again see this as a whole, such total impression cannot happen often, it is like a picture of hope. I began to call out to the other slaves, "There is hope, there is hope, we can work for Being." They crowded around in fear and tried to quiet me. "You must not speak of it aloud, they will kill us." I went on crying loudly until an old slave pushed through the crowd and took my hand and led me to the bottom of the steps. He asked the others to gather round and we all sat down in a circle about him. We were now sitting at the bottom of the steps, invisible to the audience. Then in a quiet voice, so that no one else would hear him, the old man began to address us. "Is there anyone here," he said, "who can say he knows what is meant by love of God?"

This dream only increased my trouble. It was precise in its symbolism, it pictured my stranded state. I began to compose self-indictments: "Why don't I know what to do? The answer must be that I don't believe in these ideas enough, or that I am no longer capable of acting on my beliefs. Why don't I believe enough? I am convinced that nothing else makes sense. If I continue to ask 'Does anything make sense?' I know that asking this question for years is no way of finding an answer to it. Then what in the name of sense holds me back? Why don't I begin to work? Why does the thought of it paralyze me? Why do I hold back longer than before a plunge into a cold lake?"

I could have answered that I really didn't know what to do, and could by no means find out. I knew of course that there was always a "work" to do—that difficult work of trying to "know yourself" by observing yourself. So in

Vernet I decided to perform this exercise more conscientiously.

I remembered Orage saying, "Make a list of all the
facts you know about yourself. Perhaps then you can begin
on your unknowables."

But I had made many analyses of my nature, and I asked
myself what good they did. Gurdjieff had said that one's
nature never changes; that is not the change you can affect.
I knew that really to observe yourself scientifically, you
were supposed to do another kind of examination. It consisted of not thinking, not feeling, but trying to *see* what
happens; not constating what you thought or felt or imagined—all this being invisible to an onlooker; but trying
to see yourself move and speak as you can see actors on a
film-screen moving and speaking.

I had conscientiously tried to do this last year, when
I was so unhappy that I no longer recognized myself. I was
at the lighthouse and every night I used to light candles
as if, while they burned, they would lighten my world. I
felt that I could almost see myself walking upstairs. The
house was cool and dark with the sadness of late summer.
I came to the three steps leading down to my room. On
the last one I stopped because I was lost in the room, as in
a forest at night. All I wanted was to sit down against a
tree. Once long ago I fainted—I was walking down a hotel
corridor when high banks of green water rose on either
side of me. For a long time I walked between them and as
I touched the doorhandle of my room the waters closed
over my head. The last thing I remembered was lying down

139

on an ocean bed. On this night at the lighthouse I kept on walking toward oblivion but came instead to a table with a candlestick on it. I lighted all the candles in the room. The windows were closed and their glass reflected candles of light on the trees outside. There were ten candlesticks— two of fluted glass standing on an old blue chest, two crystal ones on a walnut table. The rest were pewter and retained rather than gave off light. I sat down and looked about the room. Then I began to realize that I saw everything in it but myself. I saw the whitewashed walls and the red floor. I saw the white rug and the pink morning-glory curtains. I saw for the thousandth time these objects and others—books and pictures and my beach pajamas lying on the bed—but I did not yet see, even for the first time, the person sitting in the chair.

I made an effort to see this unseen person. Anyone else could see her as if she were moving on a film. I could only remember how she felt, remember certain words she said and certain things she did, but I couldn't hear her voice saying those words or see her movements as she drifted through actions which she did not know in advance she would perform. I knew—though I did not see it—that she had come and gone through this house, through a period of years, sometimes moving through a spell, sometimes through conviction and obsession, sometimes through bewilderment or outrage or despair. I was convinced that if I could actually see what she did and hear what she said I would know more about the kind of person she was and more about the trouble she was in.

140

I had come to believe that this kind of sight might help. Why did I believe it? Perhaps because people have tried everything else and nothing seems to have helped. No one has known human beings who give the impression of acting from knowledge of themselves or of other people. I didn't want my life to go the way of all life—to be born only to wander through experiences, to wonder at the sameness of those experiences, to want other experiences, to tire of wandering and wondering and wanting, to live at the end in remembrance of experiences, and to die—without wonder, memory, or experience.

I seemed to be doing just this, and yet I knew that in fact my life was changing. It was in this year at the lighthouse that the change began; it was in this year that the lighthouse itself changed for me. It became more than a place of peace, it will always remain for me a place where I left one of my selves which was to have no further life. I have an exact image of this separation, it left me with the feeling of being, from this time on, beside myself. The image came to me one night when I was very tired; sleep overcame me at dinner, I heard Jane's voice saying "Why don't you put your body down on the bed?" I remember getting up, pulling my topcoat tighter, walking a few steps to a divan and falling upon it face downward. Hours later I wakened and went upstairs to my room. As I walked up the stairs I saw a figure in a pink topcoat lying on a divan. I got into my bed, I lay down. I didn't seem to be there, at least something of me wasn't there because I kept seeing myself lying face downward, downstairs. The next morning the image persisted, it has persisted ever since—a topcoat holding a body which lay down on a bed. For me it never got up.

Life Class

7. In April we left Vernet for Paris, where I soon found a flat in the rue Casimir Périer, with a church in front of it and a garden behind. From there we began going daily to another flat, without a garden or any other saving charm, in the rue Colonel Renard, where Gurdjieff was living and teaching the small group I have spoken of.

I name this period the year of the predestined accident. It was in this year that I found an answer to my dilemma. The answer was that everything I had heard or experienced, at second hand—no matter how inspiring— had been too vague to produce either knowledge or understanding. The accident was that I happened to be in the right place, at the right time, in the right condition, to begin all over again.

Nothing could have been further from my preconception of what would happen to me, in this life class, than what actually began to happen. Nothing could have been further from my interpretations of what I had been told than what now appeared to take place. To me nothing took place— because what was taking place escaped me entirely.

I had always been impressed by Ouspensky's statement, in his *New Model of the Universe*, about the eternal questions, that "people feel it is impossible, or at any rate useless, to think of these things *simply*, but what it means to think of them *not simply* they do not know."

I now expected to be plunged at once into the un-simple, which, after assimilation by my "flashing" brain, I would understand in some unique way which I had always described as being able to understand Einstein without understanding mathematics.

Nothing like this happened. We simply went to lunch. Every day at two o'clock we gathered around a table cov-ered with foods I had never eaten before, never even seen before. I liked them but I wasn't prepared to be interested in them. Interest was demanded; not only interest but knowledge. I found this boring, I never know what I'm eat-ing anyway—I've had too much interruption in life over the quality of the butter or the preparation of the salad to be able to produce any active enthusiasm about food. I have come to the place where I eat because I'm hungry or simply because I love the ceremony of eating beautifully. The latter was inconspicuous at the table I'm describing, and the former was honored in a way I had never im-agined. Here one ate to eat, to know what was being eaten and why. As for conversation at this table, I was bewil-dered by its absence and felt called upon to do more than my share in developing the few remarks that were made. There were of course the toasts, and comments upon them, to which I listened lightly. After the silence of the first part of the meal, during which I was always very nervous, there was talk of a kind—formulations of great simplicity to which I gave little attention, judging that I had heard them before, in the first years at the Prieuré.

This first stage of my incomprehension lasted perhaps for two weeks, when I decided to take a more active part in the situation. Action to me has always meant rebellion, so now I began to express my disagreement with many of the things I heard. This did me no good. I watched my logic reduced to unimportance, as if logic were something that led nowhere. I had been prepared for this in theory, I wasn't at all prepared for it in fact. I fumed. This was my second phase and it lasted for months. I fumed at the table, at home during the rest of the day, and at least half the night. Sometimes I didn't sleep at all but spent the night composing all the protests I hoped and expected to make, but somehow never quite managed to, at the table. Something now always restrained me from speaking out my arguments. Instead of trying to find out what this was, I spent the time rebelling at the weakness of my resources. I had never felt weak before. Why was this stoppage upon me, how had it been imposed, why had I accepted it, why couldn't I overcome it? Months passed in this futility, my only effort being to arrive at a stronger presentation of my convictions, as well as my willingness to be convinced if only my arguments could be met and destroyed. I behaved as if I had never heard of Gurdjieff, his doctrine or its technique. No one could convince me that I was behaving this way. I thought I was kicking just enough to show that I was alive. As I saw later, it was much more than enough.

My third phase was a kind of muteness—fierce and also futile. Still understanding nothing, I still wanted to talk. But now I couldn't talk; because I couldn't be what is called "being yourself." I might have remembered some of those abstractions I thought I had incorporated—such as "What sign could you give to an astute psychologist that you existed, if stripped of your five senses and your personality?" But the truth was that I could remember nothing at all—my nature was on a rampage, though it seemed to me I had never been so expressionless in my life. When Georgette and others suggested that it might be well to do nothing for a while, especially to stop running around in emotional circles, I answered in astonishment that no one had ever taken any experience more calmly, that I was in fact doing nothing at all.

I was simply trying to be myself, I said, against some force which obstructed me. I felt that if I could only talk I could make myself understood. But to talk I always needed time, a working-up of emotions before words came to me, an expenditure of gestures which helped the words to well up. Since this manifestation was barred, as the most unnecessary of all the spectacles a super-psychologist needs to watch, I increased in frenzy. My brain told me that I had been more than understood from the beginning; but my brain was proving to be (though I never recognized this truth I knew so well) merely muscular. Certainly I was demonstrating that my brain had nothing to do with *me*.

This phase lasted for perhaps a year. As it became more and more acute, as I began to despair, I realized that I was being helped by many efforts made toward me— small efforts and great ones. They helped me into a fourth phase. It was a silence—an easier silence. I no longer wished to speak. I knew by this time that I had nothing to say, that if I had lived from birth until the present moment without having spoken one word, the result would have been the same; I could simply have made gestures to show that my cup was not full but always running over. I no longer wanted to speak because I never knew what would come out. I felt like a choirboy whose voice was changing. When I thought I was going to say something in a deep calm voice to express deep appreciation, I heard myself saying the opposite in a high thin treble. During this period, which also lasted for months, I was fed with new material, little by little. I sometimes wakened in the night and found that I was sitting on the edge of my bed in the position of Rodin's "Thinker." But I could never remember how I got into that position or how long I had been sitting there.

During two years we went, day after day, to that same table. Day after day we were given our daily bread.

Every type at the table received the bread in a different way. No one in the group duplicated, or could really identify with, the experience of the others. Nothing could have been more divergent, for instance, than each one's attitude toward the decision of what one has to give up if one follows this "follow-me" life. I heard Jane say that one never has to give up anything one still has a place left for. I can't know about anyone else; I had to try to give up practically everything I had made a place for, and try to give up the places as well. All my places were still there and so was my talent for filling them beautifully. I suppose I will always have those places and, if I can find the strength, will always be trying to fill them with something beyond the beautiful. One thing was apparent—no one else in the group had as much of the beautiful to give up as I had. They all admitted this—some with pity, all with astonishment. Solita said she had been unhappy for years, and before knowing Gurdjieff her state had become unbearable. There was no new desolation, no stripping and cleansing, no agony of effort that she didn't welcome as a change of old pain for new. This being her condition, she was led not through pain but through a new protection, combined with an effort-to-be-made which she couldn't have accepted in advance because it was one which she could never have imagined herself able to make. But she made it.

I made my effort too, but I can't be proud of it. What I feel now is that there is no shame deep enough to cover the circumstance that the effort I had to make shouldn't have been considered effort at all—and that it was almost beyond me. But this is the story of the "doctrine"—everyman's story. This is the only testimony I can pretend to offer of a doctrine which I make no pretension of understanding in its extensions, which no one understands without being *of* it, and which it would be folly to write of in generalities. Even as I try to tell of the impact of its first dimensions I see plainly how the mystery of its extension is designed for discovery. As a baby you learn to speak before you go to school, you employ the mystery of language before you begin to study the construction of the mystery.

So when I began on *a b c* it was on a parallel with my first a b c's—I was impatient, they were unnecessary, I already knew how to speak, why study what I could already accomplish?

Nevertheless I began to "study." As a person of decision I now found myself rushing through such rapids of indecision that I was always over the dam before I had come to any decision at all. As an efficient person I was now kept fumbling and dawdling before situations which I could have dispatched with a turn of the wrist. I felt that I was always standing on one foot, waiting to put down the other foot when I was given permission, or when I could be sure of getting it down. I began to hold back my whole nature for fear it wouldn't be un-manifest enough to be invited to the table. Nothing seemed to go right unless I felt hangdog. I used to walk through the streets saying "I *feel* hangdog, I *am* hangdog, I must *be* hangdog or I'll rush in where I fear to tread."

As a person of order—ah, that was the straw that broke me. At the table, as I began to recognize the order and ceremony which propelled the doctrine's presentation, my necessity for a parallel surface order became more obsessive than ever. I began to organize my life to receive the doctrine. I planned. At noon I would ask a question and hope for an answer then instead of returning for it at five o'clock, thus breaking the concentration of my day. I would write my book in the mornings, thus earning money to keep alive for a study of the doctrine in the afternoons. I would keep my evenings for a study of the sciences I had always evaded. But morning, afternoon and evening no longer held their positions, my relation to them was that of a wild comet—I never knew where I might strike. And

I was so dull about this situation of chaos that I never recognized it as order—the only order for the situation of transition.

As I began to understand the nature and purpose of the experience I was experiencing it was easier to understand what to do. And harder to do it.

The elements of my personal universe—music, love, nature and ideas—were slowly evolving. As for my ideas, I saw that they might as well have been made of paper for all the purpose they had served. As for love—of love, art, nature—I began to know that this is not the love which helps you to change your position.

Now that I had a speaking-acquaintance with this life-for-a-life material I tried to make a friend of it. My love of nature and art remained to be revised. As for nature, it had always been there, to take or to leave. But my attitude had always been an epicurean one—I had to take time to feast upon it beautifully. "Oh," I used to say to Orage, "I love the earth." "Don't talk like that," he said. "Some men love the earth, as father loves child or child father; you're only in love with it."

I could accept this evaluation, but what could I do about it? A day lived in nature, in my own way, had always seemed infallible to me . . . The rhythm of a day. I never know a day is a day unless I live it from morning till night in my own rhythm. It rains. I have several ways of feeling rain fall upon my life, as if registered by a sensitive scientific instrument. There is the first feeling— simply, the calm rain falls; the second feeling—it falls

149

and I am in it, appreciating it; the third—it rains and a conception of a day-of-falling-rain occupies me, as if I could put it to music. If I have the day free before me I feel that I experience rain. If I must do an errand at ten o'clock I cannot even feel the second-depth feeling—some flutter in me puts the experience aside, it would be too wounding to leave it, the recording-instrument would break.

If I can stay quiet, a day of sun is like a radio to me. The sun tunes in, the earth rings, boats croon down the river, I hear every sound of the day from the movement of a leaf to the flight of a fly. THIS is a day, this is a heavenly day, I am part of a heavenly day. My breathing is deep and quiet, light rises and falls, a slow magnetism flows between me and the hours.

Then there is the swift magnetism of my relation to swiftly moving things. I know it is an adrenal rhythm but it makes me feel as if I were a humming bee. Or a humming motor, ready for concentrated flight . . . I remember a silent night when I sat in a car beside a driver whose glands didn't move to my tempo. My adrenals started that increasing hum. I must get my hands on the wheel, I must, I must, a rhythm will begin, something will release the energies of another body. I heard Solita say, "Do you want to drive?" She stopped the car. I got out, got in, took the wheel. I didn't know the car, its gears were the opposite of mine, but this didn't matter, I needed to think to balance the vibration of feeling. My hands touched the wheel and a contact currented between the motor's electricity and my own. Together they established a flight. My hands lifted above the wheel as if two electricities were running—one toward sky, one into earth. The car and I, humming, trapezed through the night. There was no moon—except Venus on my left, unmoving above the rushing fields . . .

From this life of flight, attunement, fine adjustment, I now turned toward what I called life without nature—animate or inanimate. My Gurdjieffian days were broken by errands of all types—vertical lines cutting across my horizontal plane. My days felt like barbed wire . . . In town, in the middle of July, walking through the noxious gases of the exhaust pipes of automobiles, my throat burning, my ears crackling with the loudspeaker city, my head fainting with fury, my heart failing, my eyes trying not to see what they saw but, instead, distant hills. What's wrong with nature as an environment for man? I shrieked to myself, from block to block. I'm an expert in life, I have a lighthouse where all is balm and a forest where the wind runs like water. Must I "follow" through this city hell? Is it necessary? Is it right? Is it good? I'm clever enough to triumph over circumstances, why not "help others" to find lighthouses and flats with gardens? There's nothing left of me anyway except this cleverness, why not put it to use? Must we all eat burning food in a burning flat and walk the burning streets to develop a soul?

Every day I had a new rebellion . . . So this is the higher life! I said. I should think that if any life could produce authentic neurasthenia it would be just this unmanaged, mismanaged, straggling, squirming, torturing, uninteresting, uninspired succession of days that now present themselves to my numbed personality. I once saw a film of a black-sheep child. She said, "I can do what you want if I can be boss." So the intelligent teacher allowed her to boss and the child's life took on direction and inspiration. She saved herself, the school and her parents. I have always felt like this kind of child. I felt it now stronger than ever.

To turn my back on nature was hard enough, but to do it to art was, I feared, beyond me. If you could know the objective of such efforts beforehand, and their revision later, you could make them more easily. And without effect.

I had always lived on music, I wanted to hear it always, I venerated music, I think I thought that love of music was a measure of the soul's stature. When people told me that I knew nothing of reality I answered that reality was my greatest enemy, that I had fought it—successfully—all my life. My idea of what life should be was perfectly illustrated by those pictures of Beethoven playing to his friends, who sat listening with their heads bowed in their hands. I was always seeking the emotion which would allow me, compel me, to put my head in my hands. Life was never life to me unless my heart stood still.

It is like pushing aside golden clouds, trying to remember how I tried to come out from behind all this dazzlement. Even today when I suddenly hear a phrase of great lyrical music I hear myself thinking: life is music, can there be anything greater? I gather my whole organism together as if it were all needed to celebrate this glory, I listen as if listening would take me to some other sphere, I go through the complete process of hereditary build-up: is it possible I'm hearing anything so beautiful? can anything so beautiful really have been written? what did Chopin feel when he wrote it? I must arrange to hear it again right away, fortunately I can continue to hear it in memory, this is the miracle of life—that we have such memory. I felt that all people who didn't live in this state were without blessing and that they must be helped into it. I sometimes tried to decide which state—love (romantic love) or music—I could relinquish if allowed only one. For some reason I could never explain I always decided that I would have to give up love. Perhaps because one can arrange to have music continually; love isn't always available and it is so often unmusical. I played the piano under such a hypnosis of feeling that my eyes often closed under the weight of vibrations. I felt that I was accumulating more than I could use. I can't imagine, now, why this activity appeared to me like generation rather than depletion.

During 1936-38 I tried to stop living as if in emulation of Rachmaninoff's "Second Piano Concerto." I entered what I now call the D period—depression, discouragement, disgust (of self), despair, decrepitude, destruction. Having nothing of my own left—since I no longer wanted to live to music if I could help it—I began to long to travel. I made lists of all the places I would go. They always began with Innsbruck. I still wonder why.

Life now became a desert. I wouldn't musicalize and I couldn't travel. I wouldn't have traveled if I could, all I wanted with all my force was to get through the desert as quickly as possible. I had better keep a record of this new life, I said—the route between two worlds, heaven and hell. Everything to me now is like sitting down in the dentist's chair—the decision to sit takes all my time. I shall have to get worse, I suppose, to get better . . . I drift out to dinner with another ghost-of-herself. Our evening drops into melancholy as we sit on the terrace of the Café Voltaire, with a moon and a wine and nothing to do or say. I look at the moon and say, "Ah, how lovely," and Solita says, "Our dead world." The conversation stops. We walk home, I so tired of nothingness that I begin to whistle Schumann's "Abend," which begins on the lovely high note. I know everyone loathes whistling but I can't resist it; then I try to be nice again and pretend to be dazed by wine so that whatever I say will sound irresponsible and not like the conscious speech of a ghost. Perhaps it will sound funny and we can laugh. But we don't laugh. We stop at the Café Bonaparte and I say, "Yes, let's play the slot-machine game—it's something to do, it will keep our minds off the facts." We both work hard to win and even now I enjoy winning or losing . . . After the game there's nothing more to do, since I'm too tired to investigate an atom and too discouraged to study an embryo. We walk along the street and Solita says, "Look at the moon." I forget and say, "Ah, how lovely" and she says "Our dead world." By the time I reach home I'm groggy with non-existence. But Georgette is there to laugh at me and predict that tomorrow will be better. I laugh hysterically and take courage. But as Emma Goldman used to say, "What has this got to do with the revolution?" What has this got to do with the riddle of the universe which was my only reason for starting on this quest?

Things got better, and then worse again. If I have anything to say I might as well say it in that phrase—better then worse then better then worse.

The worst, the very worst, had to do with people. "Something is terribly wrong," I said, "either with me or with them, when people whom I know to be completely unversed in life seem to get on more intelligently with this new life than I do." Since they did, how could I trust the new life? People whose perceptions seemed to me so blunted that I wouldn't trust them to detect the difference between a horse and a cow in a field—how was it that they seemed to understand the meaning of this doctrine better than I did? I had always rejected such people in life—they knew none of the things I knew; now I saw them outstripping me and I couldn't stand it. What were they perceiving that I wasn't? What was the value of the thing perceived since their perceptions were of such a crude nature? But I didn't hate these people, I envied them; I didn't grow bitter, I simply admitted that I was stupider than they. This attitude was the only quality I showed that I didn't have to be ashamed of afterward.

The next phase was nausea . . . I woke in the morning feeling seasick. Nothing to do, that I *could* do, made me bilious. I felt that I was deep yellow, I hated everything I loved. All my life I've had experience with physical nausea; in the long period that precedes release I pass

through a list of rejections of all that I love and now hate
—pianos, trees, ideas. Now I felt deep yellow in an environment of deep black. If I could only go back to feeling
"normal" and work at something—houses, plans, piano,
book—what HAVE I worked at so hard (easily) all my
life? WHAT plans? I can't remember. WHAT was I working at? One would have thought, at least, the Golden Gate
bridge.

I now evaluated all my much-ado-about-something as
nothing. I had nothing that I could respect. I even began
to hate my face-expression. I may have been a darling of
the gods—that was my trouble. I saw no good in the face-
expression of a darling. I wished that I might have begun
this experience far beyond the status of a darling. Still,
I now understood enough to know that it doesn't matter
where you begin, the thing is to begin; advantages are always offset by disadvantages, everyone starts equal before
a unique activity.

To understand—that was the necessity. Understand
your nature and the nature of your type. All the qualities
which had composed "our" superiority now emerged as un-
related to that need of being born again. Our imaginations
had been the excess of desire over ability. Our intelligence
had been merely a justification of this excess. Our intense
emotions had amounted to the pleasure of having emotions.
Our art had been a hope of repeating those emotions forever. Our "rich" personalities had been an obstacle to understanding these facts. We who had been born outside the
dull, the routine, the conflicting; we the convinced, the

convincing; we the inspired, the inspiring—what had we been all our lives? Almost nothing at all. We were balloons that had got up to the ceiling and stayed there because we couldn't get any higher. We had considered ourselves Nietzchean transvaluers of all values, but all we had really done was to act like Gabriele D'Annunzio.

Georgette as usual had a picture of our plight. "We have spent our lives walking about under parasols," she said. Yes, I thought—white silk parasols, like those used by Catholics in midnight Mass at New Year's.

From now on I had a more concrete picture of the soft past and the hard future. Each period always seemed an end and always proved to be only a beginning. To the end of life, I suppose, this will be my condition of life. There was the abstract period, the stable-cleaning period, the camel-through-the-needle's-eye period, the rat-on-the-wheel period—the impulse, the decision, the effort, the work, the fluctuation, the rebellion, the recession, the new decision, the new effort. I now saw that if you can manage to qualify, something will be revealed to you. The more you can qualify the more you will be invited to qualify. This will go on until the rat-on-the-wheel situation has attained its zenith. Then if it's in you to keep on turning, you stay on the wheel. But the wheel is not merely the wheel of life, nor is it Ouspensky's New Model of the Universe. It is another formula.

8. It had taken me a long time to find out what I was finding out day by day. It had been a long time since I had remembered my life year after year. My years were no longer chronological or pictorial, they were not a passage of time but a passage from one accretion to another. A year was now worth no more than its formulations. I no longer said "Remember the year when we first heard Stravinsky's 'Sacre'?" or "That was the year of the nightingale." I now said, "Remember the year when I was told 'You rest in dream'?" These four words—so simple, said so long ago—are the only direct words of Gurdjieff to me that I have quoted in this book.

And I remember the year when I could at last formulate "I am empty." I remember my first horror and incredulity as I screamed (to myself) *"I* empty? I who have always been so interested in the nature of the universe?"

Then I remember the day when, suddenly, I had no more screaming to do, only cracking. There were guests for lunch that day, at Gurdjieff's table. Among them was one from the old days at the Prieuré, one who should have known from the beginning that "Gurdjieff is not a single man but a multitude, and through the multitude there walks a sage; in his talk there is always teaching; you must watch for it, you must not be put off." This woman appeared not to know it, or not to want to know, or not to want to show that she knew. I may misjudge her, but I could only believe that she didn't know. And when she said, "Good heavens, the same old repertoire, I don't see how you stand it day after day," I felt that she didn't even

158

suspect what was taking place. In the repertoire that day, when none of the guests seemed to be listening, six words were said to me—placed formally in the informal talk. After lunch the unsuspecting guest said, "Was that a special crack you got?" "Oh no," I said. One of the less unsuspecting said, "Don't take it too hard, whatever it was." "Oh no," I said, "it was just a hint."

It had been a revelation. For the first time I knew that my shell had cracked open. For the first time I saw that I was as stupid as I was vain, and as egotistic as I was empty.

9. It was afternoon when the lighthouse emerged for us, again, from its trees and the river. The tide was high, birds were singing, flowers blooming, the sun and air and earth received us again for another summer.

Inside I looked once more at the rooster plates, and the cracked ones with roses. Ten years had passed since we first came here and everything was the same. I walked up the spiral stairs. I walked down the three steps to my room and opened the windows. Air from the forest entered. I sat down. Everything was the same. But I was not.

I had always been the same before, no matter what had happened to me or in me or around me. What could I say to anyone who asked me what change was, or why I was changed, or what I thought had changed in me? I tried to formulate the hair's-breadth difference which would contain the meaning. I would say = I now have something which no page of philosophy, psychology, cosmology, physics, chemistry, geology, biology, astronomy, astrology, microscopy, mathematics, metaphysics, magic or mysticism could have given me. They would say = But the Bible? No, I would say, no page of Bible. They would say = What can Gurdjieff give that the Bible doesn't give? I would say = Everything. The Bible doesn't give it, only shows it. No words on paper can give you anything except what you yourself make them give. You can't make them give enough. You can make them give you a faith. That is a great deal. It is not enough, since there is something more.

I could hear the voices of millions of preachers sending out their Sunday words over radios—"Have faith." I suddenly heard Bach composing "I call upon Thee, Jesus" —because he *had* faith. I suddenly heard a simple man telling of the white light that shines for him around the words "Do unto others as you would have others do unto you." I remembered all the voices from my past. "Can't you just accept the fact that there is Something and stop worrying?" "No," I always said. "Can't you accept an hypothesis, as a scientist does, and go along with it until it gives out?" "No," I said. "Why not?" "Why should I? We already know where all the hypotheses have given out." "Can't you just have faith in God and rest on that?" "No," I said.

Faith in God. You understand what faith is, you try to understand what God is. I thought about the St. Paul type of faith—that conviction of faith in faith. I thought about another type of faith—that conviction of the un-

160

known knowable. I wondered how this faith could be put
into words on paper. I would begin by stating the subject.
The subject is: the nature of the human soul and its fate
—without, or with, cultivation. If I were allowed only a
few sentences to develop such a subject, I would choose a
summary once made by Solita: "There is a force in man
which natural man does not develop. This force, known to
Hermetic science, is the 'life of men'—the essence of that
mystical vine of which we are the branches—without which
there could be no consciousness at all. Humanity unaided
can never find this secret, it must be initiated into the super-
natural principle which man has within him, which scientifically is called the 'life principle' without the scientists
or religionists suspecting what it is they call 'life.' The
real religion communicates only two commands to the
world, over and over, for the few who wish to be chosen—
'As above so below' and 'You must be born again.' For
rebirth there is an exact science, the greatest in the world
and sacredly concealed. Why? If it were told what would
become of the law: Seek and you will find?"

I went on thinking of how this knowledge can be
learned, of the conditions in which it can be communicated,
of the method of its communication: no information that
goes into the mind alone; no stimulation for the mind
which will merely leave you satisfied with stimulation; no
stimulation for your feelings which will leave you content
merely to feel; no rewards for the personality; no great
revelations—until they take place. And on your part: no
mere taking thought; no withdrawal from the world; no
sacrifices too great to make—once you have made them;

161

no impasses of time, or money, or need to earn your daily bread—they must be or will be or can be resolved. And if you don't find a Gurdjieff? You do—if you search.

I saw the evolution of man in a new picture—as long as a million years of the evolution of a universe. I saw every phenomenon turning on that hair's-breadth difference which becomes—creation. I saw a long cord from womb to womb, and another from "self" to "self."

I saw myself—no longer sitting on a cloud; nor was I left sitting on the ground. I was no longer unhappy, nor would I be happy again. I would never again be anything but rejoicing. A blessing was upon me, I felt it on every side. I would no longer be spared, or killed, or protected. I would be helped. Years will pass and I know what I will be doing. I do not know where I will live, what I will eat or wear, how I will look or "feel," or whom I shall be seeing. In the world there will be war, in my world there will be no peace—except that which passes understanding: a lifetime for a life—for "what abides shining, not burning, as below, or wrathful; but vital, calm, transmuting, recreating, and no longer a consuming fire."
Paris, March, 1938.

2. WAR
and our World

...A cool and quiet June in the rue Casimir Périer. Paris was still, with the calm that precedes a storm . . . or a war; even talk of war was for the moment in suspension. We were ready to leave for the lighthouse, yet lingered on in the charm of a city waiting for summer. The sycamore trees swayed in our windows all day and at evening enclosed us in a wood. I often went to sit in the little park of Ste. Clotilde, beside the statue of César Franck who was once the organist of this tall grey church. Sometimes I sat on the café terrace facing the south portal and wondered if war was really about to strike the world's immortal city.

It was the brightest morning in June and Georgette stood before her mirror. I heard her calling to Monique. There was a silence, then I heard her say, "Look at this curious little swelling. I wonder what it is."

I went into her room. "Evidently it is nothing," Georgette was saying, "but it is rather curious." Foreboding blacked out the room for me. "No," I heard myself saying, "it is just a little swelling, it couldn't mean anything."

The next day, at the American Hospital, Dr. Thierry de Martel told Monique and me that it meant . . . what we had suddenly, terribly and unaccountably feared.

He told Georgette that she had an innocuous tumor, which, if not removed, might become malignant. She believed just one word of this diagnosis—"innocuous"—since she always believed only what seemed to her *à propos*. Malignancy wasn't *à propos* and she refused an operation.

2. Thus on a June Day, in 1939, our exemption came to an end.

Thus, without the slightest sign of illness, without a trace of warning pain . . . within twenty-four hours, on a cloudless summer day, by the merest accident of a glance in a mirror—an observation, a question, an examination, a verdict . . . our world stood still facing a word—cancer.

We didn't believe it. We couldn't believe it—it was too sudden. We wouldn't believe it—it was too monstrous. And Georgette herself never believed it.

Even after she consented to an operation, and later when her arm began to swell, she believed the cause was a stoppage in the circulation, due to a severed muscle. People told us that she "knew," that she hid her knowledge from us. She would have been expertly capable of this. But we knew that she didn't know. Only a month before her death, two years later, she called out one day in a ringing voice—she was standing at the top of a stairs—"Come quickly—you see this new symptom?—it means that my arm is getting well. I *know* now this is the beginning of my *guérison.*" The new symptom was the beginning of the end.

A week before her death, when she realized at last that she was dying, she asked Monique, "Could this be cancer?—have the doctors said that?" When Monique said "No" and gave a technical explanation, she accepted it. Perhaps at that moment she knew. If she did, it no longer mattered to her. By that time she had only one thought: how to prepare herself to meet death. She talked only of Gurdjieff and his doctrine. She tried with all the forces still intact in her to apply it to the last days and moments of her life.

After that June day Monique and I knew that we were facing two wars—the war men would fight against Hitler, the war we would fight against cancer. We didn't believe we were losing our war until the very end. And not even then . . .

For twenty-eight months we fought with every resource we had, and with others we discovered. First, we had to conceal our grief; second—and the doctors agreed —we had to conceal our knowledge. This was not difficult; we found so many ways . . . and no one could have helped us more than Georgette herself. Doctors could tell her anything, medically, and she would believe them—if they told her intellectually.

Georgette had always been the kind of person with whom great doctors have great conversations. They would quickly switch their facts from the physiological to the

psychological; a discussion of the miracle of the circula-
tory system would lead them to the miracle of the
sympathetic nervous system, and from there to endless
speculation on "man the unknown." All French doctors of
any note are willing to use science to prove the existence
of what is beyond their knowledge. This is what Georgette
needed and got from them. There could be no more ideal
conversations, for her, than those she could have with
Dr. Pierre Lecomte du Noüy, a life-long friend.*

What the doctors got from Georgette was an authentic
and poetic documentation of her inner-world states. At this
time she was finishing her book, *La Machine à Courage*.†
In it she had written a chapter on her "struggle with death"
during pneumonia. One of her eminent doctor friends
loved to discuss these findings with her. He said, "It is as
if, through the intuitions of poetry, you had penetrated
into the secret life of the cells."

But Georgette was now engaged in a struggle which
she described as "less natural" than that against death—
the struggle against "dying before one's death." The later
years of her life, under Gurdjieff, had been dedicated to
this struggle, and in the last section of her book, which she
called "A Well of Water," she was working out a problem:
how to write of the "living water" she had received from
Gurdjieff. Her testimony to the words, "But whosoever
drinketh of the water that I shall give him shall never
thirst; but the water that I shall give him shall be in him

* Author of *Human Destiny*.
† Published posthumously by J. B. Janin, with a preface by Jean
Cocteau, in Paris in 1947.

168

a well of water springing up into everlasting life," and her effort to formulate it, occupied the two years of her illness. That is why she, and even we, sometimes forgot that she was ill.

Just yesterday I read, with a special sadness, this passage in the *Journals* of André Gide, written in 1937:

"I tell myself that it is probably not bad that there should withdraw from us progressively the earth one would have too much trouble leaving—that one would have too much trouble leaving all at once. The wonderful thing would be, at the same time, to get progressively nearer to . . . . something else."

Gide was sixty-eight when he wrote these words. Georgette was the same age when she wrote of having found "something else." She used the same term—"*autre chose.*" And four years later, as she lay dying, she was still living in that prophecy of a well of water springing up into everlasting life. Her last conscious words were: "*Alors, nous allons mourir sans mourir?*"

3. During July and August of 1939 Georgette held out against an operation. Then as war approached, at the end of August, she consented—as if private surgery seemed more appropriate to her in a time of public slaughter.

Dr. de Martel didn't believe war was coming. "It's not for this year," he said; "I'll operate Thursday at the American Hospital."

We reserved a room for Wednesday. On that morning the first troops were called up and we cancelled the room—Georgette couldn't face an operation under bombing. "I still don't think we'll have war," Martel said, "but if you're nervous I'll operate later."

Georgette wasn't nervous, she was panic-stricken. For three years she had been aghast at the coming war. Now, overnight, she believed, as most people did, that as soon as France mobilized the Germans would bomb Paris.

By the end of the week the American Hospital began its planned evacuation to Etretat, on the Normandy coast. Martel said he would operate there, and we prepared for flight from Paris. For a week our car, and those of our American friends, had been ready—three cars full of winter clothes, books, typewriters, manuscripts, radios; every inch of space had been measured for utility, we had all agreed to take no luxuries or personal treasures. But I said to myself, "I'm not yet taking orders from the Gestapo," and I kept a free place for something that had become a part of our lives: Rachmaninoff's "Second Piano Concerto," * played by the composer and Stokowski—a brown album that fitted exactly under the seat. *"C'est trop beau,"* Georgette always said over the opening chords, as her eyes became blind with listening.

Though there was no need to hurry, as we saw later, we left Paris as if it were already under martial law, as if we had only an hour for escape. Our destination was Tancarville, for a few days' rest; then Etretat. We were tense in the car, thankful for every kilometre gained

* It had not yet been done to death by America.

170

without being halted . . . imaginary dramas of pursuit and capture that mark a war's beginning. My own chief fear was that our car would be requisitioned. We drove up the Champs Elysées, out the Avenue de la Grande Armée which, on my first day in Paris, I had misread as Grande-Aimée—(what a romantic country! I had thought). At St. Germain we stopped at a café facing the château and the station, bought *Paris Soir* and the *Herald Tribune*. The town had changed overnight — people stood about in the streets reading newspapers, soldiers with determined faces walked with aimless feet, a fat woman in the bakery told me about the last war. "Soldiers came in every day from the front, we met their trains. It was terrible the way they begged for soap, but most of all they wanted handkerchiefs, even the badly wounded seemed to suffer less when they could wipe their faces with something clean." We went back to the car, ashamed of its beauty, ashamed of the fresh white handkerchiefs in the side pocket where I had put them that morning.

At seven we drove in to Orgeval, a village thirteen kilometres beyond St. Germain, and decided to wait there with our friends for developments. We waited for a week, while the nations decided for or against war. The inn and our friend's house were full of French officers, some of them volunteers of sixty, still gallant and vital with coquetry—one a marquis-captain with eyes of such deep personal incertitude that you wondered how he was to command other men. We stood around the radio to get news from London and New York on the short waves. We were all in that state of nervous excitement that can't

171

be controlled. Everyone coming out from Paris brought news as you bring candy to your hostess, and the one who predicted that Paris would be bombed that night became the most exciting guest. The town-crier came, beating his drum, to order all windows covered with blue paper so that no crack of light might be visible to an enemy plane.

In the daytime we bought provisions—candles, matches, sugar, soap, cotton, iodine, aspirin, toothpaste. At night we walked in the fields. The moon, Jupiter, Venus and Mars had come together in the sky that month, like an omen—or a warning. Would the life we had known in Europe be destroyed? Would this war start a world involution? Were we ourselves destined to become catastrophe-people? Could we stay together or would we be separated? Should those who had resources go back to America, try from there to rescue the others? And Georgette?—what was to come for her? We talked of these things under the stars, under the ominous group of planets and the moon. But more often we didn't talk; we walked and looked and listened, measured the peace and order of night. What peace? Stars living and dying . . .

And in this same mysterious dissolution, Georgette doomed mysteriously to die.

At the end of the week we left for Tancarville. At Bolbec, driving into the square, we looked for the cat in the café window—the remembered annual picture: cream and white house, red geraniums, grey cat sleeping in the sun.

Tancarville too was unchanged . . . autumn had come again to the château. I walked through the corridor, straightened the *Richelieu,* stopped as usual to look at the picture beside it—St. Mars walking to the scaffold— and to wonder, as one does through a lifetime, how a man feels as he walks to his death. In my old room, No. 9, I lay on the bed and sank into the baseless peace that comes after grief too long concealed. Outside my windows the Seine—sky, river, timbered hills, meadows with cows, rooks flapping and calling as they did in my first autumn here, sixteen years ago. *Rien n'a donc changé . . . que nous.*

We stayed for two nights, then started out for Etretat. As we came into Criquetot and turned to the right before the church, sirens began to wail. Georgette thought it was a bombardment; it was, at last, the announcement of mobilization. The sun was bright on the church; when the sirens stopped the air throbbed with silence. We drew up to the sidewalk. People were coming out of their houses as if on strings that pulled them to the café. They stood staring at nothing and saying, *"C'est la guerre."*

Etretat . . . a large cool village for summer, deserted now in autumn mists; pine trees and sea and sheep on green grass against grey water; the American Hospital just entering the Golf Hotel, confusion and efficiency, patients from Neuilly already in their new quarters, hundreds of nurses; the market-place already invaded by Americans from Paris, cocktails at tables in the square before the ancient and beautiful market-house; in our hotel a Polish woman who feared that her house in Krakow had been destroyed, since it stood beside the Parliament buildings just bombed by the Germans.

Saturday night, September 2. Georgette calm, as always when disaster has been fully stated. She asked for no music on the radio, but only to sleep. Perhaps to dream, I found myself saying—she who dreamed so often of youth and spring. I played the radio in my room, then stood on the balcony, hearing the dark sea and its rhythms, faint, regular and hard. Perhaps one day both war and cancer would be obsolete . . .

Sunday morning, September 3. Eleven o'clock. We sat by the radio, waiting for Chamberlain. The sea was high, waves boomed between his phrases—"England is now at war with Germany." At the end he said, "We shall be fighting evil things." Then the PTT radio station played a Chopin polonaise. On all the following days news bulletins were prefaced by Chopin—preludes, etudes, waltzes, mazurkas. The war for me became a victory, known in advance—Chopin over Hitler.

Dr. de Martel was mobilized, couldn't leave Paris; his operating equipment might not be installed in Etretat for several weeks. Dr. Fuller examined Georgette. "It's developing very fast," he said, "you must have the operation immediately."

There was nothing to do but return to Paris where Martel would operate in his own *clinique* in the rue Vercingetorix, since the American Hospital had already been taken over by the army.

Back in Paris, Saturday September 9, late afternoon; up the three flights of stairs — the church a soft shadow in our windows. We had dinner under the yellow lamp and didn't know it was to be our last dinner in this place where we had faced together the "changing course" of our lives under the great hand of Gurdjieff. Here we had also faced other, lesser illnesses. Monique and I sat beside Georgette's bed, smiling, until she fell asleep. Then we sat together in the next room for a long time.

Sunday—Martel's *clinique*. Blood tests. Monday morning Georgette's arm black from elbow to shoulder from the long needles. As night came on I could only watch her face, sense the assemblage of all her forces for the next day's ordeal. I knew she had no need to speak; for me, I had only to imagine one of those great statements of hers, so precise and heartbreaking, which made you sure that no experience in life, even that of death, would find her a stranger to it.

Tuesday morning. We stood beside the bed as a nurse gave her morphine. It didn't work quickly; we walked beside her concentrated face as the stretcher was rolled through corridors.

The operation took a long time. When we were allowed to go into her room I saw her arm strapped to the bed-rail behind her head. She looked just past my eyes and said, *"J'ai si mal"* . . . of all human words perhaps the most difficult to endure.

"I got it all out," Martel said. But he didn't say it wouldn't come back. His face, as he shook our hands, was as concentrated as a knife.

I had a cot put in Georgette's room and lay there through the night listening for air-raid alarms. They came the second night. I kept Georgette from hearing them by talking of the lighthouse; I could feel her smiling in the dark. When the nurse came to take us down to the shelter she heard Georgette saying *"Comme c'est beau,"* and she left us in peace.

Paris under a black-out—I could scarcely see my way through the streets as I drove back and forth from the *clinique.* Some people had gas masks, not furnished by the government as in England but bought from it, if you were lucky enough to have a head size the government considered normal. I came within this category, but both Georgette and Monique had smaller heads for which no provision had been made. Somehow I never believed in my mask and never tried to put it on.

Our American friends decided to leave for New York, then send for us as soon as Georgette could travel. I drove to Orgeval to say goodbye. We had breakfast at five in the morning, started out at five-thirty through a countryside lost in fog and said our farewells at a cross-roads. We were like figures in an old engraving, parting at dawn on dangerous missions, but with motorcars instead of horses standing in the mist. We were all so stupe-fied by events that we felt no emotion at all.

Twelve days after the operation Georgette left the *clinique.* Instead of going to our flat—which was behind the Chambre des Deputés and a perfect bomb target—we stayed for a week at a small left-bank hotel for which we had a tenderness. The little proprietor felt it necessary to calm Georgette about a German invasion. "What if the Germans do come to Paris, madame?" he said with powerful gestures. "What if they come to this hotel? I will meet them at the door and I will stop them. I will say, *'Messieurs, je suis chez moi.'* "

The end of September . . . and the last time I saw Paris. But this is not a true thing to say. I never stopped seeing Paris.

It was a day like white wine and we started out again for Tancarville. I remember the happiness of this day—the success of the operation, the paralysis of the war, the prospect of familiar roads through villages and farmlands; our arrival at the château where a *valet de chambre* in his white coat would be standing on the *perron* ringing the first bell for dinner; we would have just time to look at our rooms again, then assemble before the fire in the salon where, long since, electricity had replaced the kerosene lamps.

But there was no one about as we drove in. We went upstairs and from far down the corridor someone waved us back. Five minutes later a servant came to tell us that "monsieur" had just died—the man who never moved and who read books about energy.

No undertaker was called, the servants tied a handkerchief underneath his chin, his *legion d'honneur* was put in his buttonhole and a cross in his hands, thus composing the final picture of a man who had never made a selfless gesture in his life. Every time I met his wife in the halls during the next two days she was carrying still another cross to put beside him. "I love the cross," she said. I couldn't imagine what she meant—she had never spoken of it before, during a lifetime.

In a long procession, led by the villagers, we drove up the hill to the church. A choir of old men with white moustaches wheezed through the service. These singers replaced younger men who had been mobilized; throughout a war they remained at the disposal of the dead in all the villages of France. They looked like walruses, they threw back their heads and sang with a snarl, like dogs wrestling with seaweed on a beach; an organist played with one finger on a portable organ placed in the aisle, and neither he nor the organ nor the singers had any liking for tune or time. The rasping ceremony lasted for an hour and a half. At the grave a priest paid tribute to "this gentle, discreet man loved by all, whose bounty both private and public is so well known." Then the mayor, holding a paper in his trembling hand, turned to the coffin with intimate words: *"Cher monsieur,* rest in peace"—which was what monsieur had done all the days of his life.

October came and Georgette's wound hadn't healed. We were told this was a bad sign. We had a good doctor in Tancarville and I wondered whether we shouldn't stay there for the war's duration. It was still important to me that we should be in a beautiful place; in our desperation I felt we would somehow be sustained by landscape and architecture. Besides, there were forests and thick-walled ruins for shelter from bombs, wood for fires, gardens for food. If the Normandy winter was severe we could exercise by walking the endless corridors, as on shipboard.

I counted the steps along the upper hall—151. You could do a mile by walking it several times.

October was a month of stupor—I could do nothing but read detective stories. I had brought twenty of them from Paris, and as the neurasthenic days passed into twilight I shut myself in my room, escaping war and illness by concentrating on crime. I read into the night, hating myself, shocked at the distance I saw between my present state and last year's elevations. What had become of that other life—"vital, calm, transmuting, recreating, and no longer a consuming fire"? Now there was not even the consuming fire, there was nothing. I had again become nothing—because I could not face life without the presence of the symbol it had offered me—the symbol that Georgette represented—the perfect human being. What would life be like under a lower order? The life of people. How could I live it? What would people want of me or I of them? In my helpless grief I rejected in advance the character of the world itself. I had lived for twenty years in the presence of a "saint of lyricism"; must I now enter the movement and mutter of a daily world?

For the thousandth time I asked myself what was taking place in that lyric spirit, immobile in the next room, its visible form inert on a bed, in pain, facing what unknown realms of greater pain and pre-determined courage? I knew what was taking place. If I should stop my drugged pursuit of crime, hurl my detective stories through the window and walk into the next room, I knew what I would see and hear. Georgette would be lying against her pillows, she would look at me and say, "But, *chérie,* we must think only of that *other thing*—a life for a life." She was still trying, I had stopped trying. I was headed toward an involution. Must I touch its depth before I could again begin a new beginning? I feared the answer was yes.

I didn't go into the next room but I did stop reading, and I did begin to think, and I wrote down in rushing words all that I could formulate about the life of people that we had never lived. Analyze, I said to myself, the benediction that has been upon you all these years; write it down and then reread the words every day to produce courage, because merely to read of such a benediction is a power, a protection, a source. Even after Georgette dies it will carry on its meaning in some unknown way. I remember all that I said to myself that night, all that I would forever say if anyone asked me, "What blessing are you talking of that you think is unknown to us? Don't we all have it, from someone, even if we live the uninspired life of people?" No, no, no, I would answer and maintain. You do not have it because it is based on a word you do not understand. That word is freedom, the unknown freedom, the kind people seem to live without. You may have the four freedoms, and others, and then what do you have besides? Nothing and nothing and nothing of what I am talking about. Define it then, I kept saying to myself; define this undreamed-of, unconceived human freedom that exists nowhere as far as your eyes can see; describe this universe of human perfection in which you have lived and which you will never find again in the capacities of other human beings. Georgette, Monique and I free in our fabricated world—no strangers to trouble, but all our trouble the kind that can be dealt with: no trouble except the right kind: not conflict but struggle—the struggle that is generative. All the rubble and underbrush, the confusion of human complexes out of the way to begin with. That is all I want to say: we have had a classic life.

It is different, I said, from any other life I have ever seen. The basis of it is freedom from talk, talk, talk; freedom from the greeds, groans and gesticulations of the human animal; freedom from posings and posturings; freedom from comment on what you are doing, saying, feeling; freedom from words-that-must-be-retracted and scenes-that-must-be-forgiven and forgotten; freedom from what Georgette calls the "dog-to-dog of humanity." I have lived days, weeks, when I am linked, humanly, with no human being. With Georgette the place for this free place is always open. No one else has ever given me the impression of offering absolute freedom—the kind that doesn't turn on you at some moment, over some slight human snag. It is as if Georgette had lived a picture of life —a formalization. With her you can sit in a room as if no one else were there. Why can you never do this with other people? Because they are in the habit of saying something at all times. You too fall into the habit; you begin to say words in order not to appear strange, you make the expected smiles, false smiles that become grimaces, smiling at nothing like a fool—horrible—you can't stop, words come out of you as exclamations, empty as the voice that speaks them. This is communal life— it is terrifying; you can never let yourself drop into quietness, you can never hear the hum of silence that sometimes fills the world. You can never count on a sustained state for more than a minute at a time. Even an hour at a time is not enough—it must be a state that can be entered at any time. But to be interrupted, frittered, dispersed, shattered—this is considered normal. To ask for release from it is considered selfish, demanding, ivory-tower, escapist. Why? No one ever knows how many important emotions he will forget, or never have, if he lives this dispersion. I consider it vulgar for people to clamor at me, wearing me down, eating me alive. Why don't they just remain silent in my silences? Why are they always sneaking up on my vibrations? Why don't they just "sit down in a chair and exist"? I never get any rest except with Georgette. She "exists" alone; this allows me to exist alone. Her life begins where all conventional life ends. It is based on extremes: real talk or absence of talk; interest in all that you do, or oblivion to all that you do—as you prefer, you have only to ask. What am I saying? You need never ask, it is always known. Her ways are the ways of wisdom and they produce the solace of freedom of mind.

Plans are useless in wartime and ours were changed at the end of October by a telegram from Hendaye: "Have found charming villa for you, four rooms, three hundred francs a month" (about eight dollars).

We left the sheltered splendor of Tancarville for a town we didn't know but which represented hope, because it was on the Spanish border. From Hendaye you could cross a bridge to Irun, then pass through Spain to Portugal, and from there to the sanctuary of America. Georgette was sure that in New York she would find effective treatment for her inexplicable malady, as well as radio, concert and lecture engagements. She believed this unwaveringly until a month before her death.

On the way we stopped for the night at a roadside inn. Long afterward I found a description, in Georgette's little red notebook, of what happened to her there: *"Un soir de fatigue, et j'ai tant toussé que la plaie de ma poitrine s'est ouverte. Je vois ça dans la glace de l'auberge comme le sang d'un Jésus de mauvaise qualité—un Jésus de la foire. A Tancarville, malade, j'ai commencé par une souffrance personelle. J'avais bêtement peur à chaque pas. Ce mal a continué—pendant un mois j'ai vécu l'horreur dans mes veines, mes entrailles, et puis, mieux portante, le mal s'est agrandi et m'a dépassé. J'ai vécu une désespoir trop grande pour un être humain"* . . .*

The Villa Victor Marie, in Hendaye, was not charming. It was made of brick and cement; only the kitchen was sympathetic—the other rooms presented an environment which, for the first time in my life, I felt powerless to transform. Still, every room looked over the Atlantic and

---

* An evening of fatigue . . . and I coughed so much that my wound opened. Standing before the mirror of the inn, as the blood slowly flowed, I saw my image as a Jesus of inferior quality—a carnival Jesus. In Tancarville, ill after the operation, I had fallen into a state of personal anguish—at every moment, stupidly, I felt fear. That fear continued—during a month I felt horror in my veins, in my bones; and then, as I grew stronger physically, my moral suffering increased until it overwhelmed me. I lived a despair too great for a human being.

the sounds of that sea enveloped us. Hendaye has the loveliest natural *plage* in the world. Biarritz and St. Jean de
Luz are six kilometres away, Spain just across the lagoon,
marked by an old church with a beautiful tower.

I must keep a diary, I said. Entrenched in Hendaye
for the duration of the war (for how could we ever get
to America?), I would try to keep a record of what happened to us, inside and outside. We were alone in the
world, except for the friend who had found our villa (but
she was leaving) and our proprietress, who looked like a
turtle and turned out to be a trained nurse, full of kindness for us. In a far corner of the world, separated from
our kind, under menace of death, I knew that we would
begin again what Bacon called "the good days of the
mind."

4. I didn't keep a diary, I kept a vague
journal. To record facts and dates in diary form was
difficult for me. Instead of noting "Georgette better yesterday, not so well today," I found myself writing "Monique has just brought another spray of honeysuckle and
I hear Georgette's cry of delight."

That journal is a record of emotions. Yet none of
them is expressed.

Now I can express them. They are before me like a
beloved landscape which I know by heart, which I cannot
wait to look at again.

We went walking. (November 6). Nine Czech students
had just been tortured and shot, but we were free to walk

184

on a beach at sunset. The sun was pink, the mountains
blue transparencies. There was a sound of surf on a long
wide beach; pale feathery trees on an endless avenue; a
half-moon and starry lights appearing one by one on the
hill across the quiet lagoon—Font Arabie, Spain; the
church tower at the top, delicate and fancy; the quiet
wind, the smell of sea and eucalyptus, our footsteps silent
on the sand, churchbells ringing like soft songs and the
moon a pale rose framed in paler light—a *carte postale*
of divine elements.

A letter from Paris: "Life in Hendaye will be *bien morose*
for you both." We laughed. How little people know us,
we said; how happy we shall be here . . . too much to do,
too much to think about. Our conversations began.

 The first thing to remember, we said, is not to let
ourselves sink into a status-quo atmosphere of war associations. It is a madness that will pass, only to be succeeded by another. In the current madness even Hitler
isn't to blame—he's merely a tool of nature: on the theory
that Nature needs certain emanations and gets them—millions of human beings agonizing over the war—all those
vibrations filling the invisible universes. But even if you
try to live outside this pattern, can you succeed? And if
you do, can you believe that your small effort toward
"quality vibrations" will offset the gigantic push of "quan-
tity vibrations"? Tragic to be cut off from Gurdjieff. But
he said, "I have given you enough for years." We must
work out what we have been given—we will have a series
of experiences, year after year. The wish to go on, the

struggle not to fall back—all this makes a friction that produces combustion . . . and out of these energies springs a fire.

These thoughts were sometimes so strong in me that I sat up all night, rereading Gurdjieff's book. New meanings emerged.

I transformed our rooms. The one with a fireplace became a studio, with the white wool rugs and yellow château curtains (always carried in the car). I bought emerald green wrapping-paper to cover a large work table and found some white tarlatan in a village shop to make little curtains for the front windows; and put a lamp in each one so that when we walked on the beach at evening we would come back to the lighted glow of a home.

It was good not to be in Paris. No telephone rang, no one asked me to a cinema which I should have liked to see—though I was happier not knowing that I could see it; no one asked me to dine at Michaud's, which I should have loved to do—but how much more I loved being in an ugly little villa, in the circle of the evening lamp, with shadows of mountains around our world and our evening talk uninterrupted, our evening study undisturbed . . . atoms, bones and muscles and organs, drops of water, universes in every drop, in every model and conception; two forces always in operation with a third force; western science blind to the third (or neutralizing) force. Still, scientists had now discovered the neutron, the neutrino and the neutretto (??). Must discover the working of three forces in all things, in all situations, all phenomena. Most of this was beyond me—except the abstract statements. Why, oh why, hadn't I studied science when I was young?

. . . The experience of a summer night. I changed the position of my bed, to face trees instead of sea. As I was falling asleep a night insect began to sing and evoked all the summer nights of my life . . . quintessence of the spell of night . . . the sense of a planet turning from light to darkness, stars moving across the sky, insects singing in circles of sound that could be heard around the earth . . . and I walking toward a lake carrying a rose . . . because I was in love.

We went to St. Jean de Luz for X-ray treatments. Dr. de Martel insisted on them; they made Georgette super-nervous for days afterward.

We found a tea-shop there, stacked with *patisserie*. Georgette walked from counter to counter, making her grave selection. Only three—more would have been extravagant. After she had chosen she would walk through the shop again, changing a rich green cake for a richer pink one.

I remember Armistice Day. President Lebrun spoke on the radio in trembling tones; the Queen of England spoke in the sweet tones of a young girl. Englishwomen's speaking voices usually richer . . . but their singing voices!—no emptier sound exists. Comes from no training (life training) in the emotional center?—flat solar plexus, Georgette said. Like English choirboys—always one note in their voices that makes me writhe . . . that white note of sexlessness. I had to return those records of the famous English boy-choir, couldn't stand that note.

Georgette's wound healed, except for a small point. She began to eat, sleep and breathe better. She was getting well, we said; doctors didn't know everything—other people had been saved by operations, if performed in time. Monique and I learned what the word hope means.

Our life in Hendaye took on a form and rhythm. In the mornings we worked on our books; in the afternoons we walked to the cake-shop in the lovely deserted town and brought back a *gateau basque* for tea; ate it at the kitchen table, placed at a right angle to the sea which was running high on these strong autumn days. A blue sea . . . I had always thought the Atlantic was grey, compared to the Pacific or the Mediterranean; but in Hendaye it was deep blue even on days of storm.

On November 20—unforgettable day, because we had almost no money left—a check came from New York. *The Blue Bird* had just been filmed, with Shirley Temple, and Dodd Mead had brought out a de-luxe edition of Georgette's *Story of the Blue Bird*. We thought the check was for 2,830 francs—a fortune. As we gazed at it we saw 28,-300 francs!

After we came to our senses I said, "Let's spend the extra three hundred francs right away—one hundred for each of us; but on one condition: that each one does a

188

selfish thing for once without thinking of the others and without feeling extravagant."

I started out and kept the conditions easily. I spent thirty francs for chocolates—(how many years since we had known such recklessness!); ten francs for candied fruit, twenty for a bottle of Quinquina St. Raphael; an illustrated magazine and a chicken for Sunday. Monique went next and came back with three little gifts for Georgette—nothing for herself. Later Georgette strolled off to the postoffice and came back looking almost sly. She had sent off two money-orders of fifty francs each to two friends in Paris about whom she was worried. "No fair," I said, "this was to have been an egotistical day."

Determined to spend money easily, Georgette and I lunched at the Golf Hotel in St. Jean. Three Englishwomen sat at the next table and talked like this:

"Did you see So-and-So this morning?" "Yes, I saw him just as he was leaving the hotel." "*I* saw him just as we were leaving." "No, my dear, we saw him just as we were going into the chemist's, don't you remember?" "Oh yes, perhaps it was then—yes, I believe it was then, after all." "Yes, I think it was." "Isn't Mary coming down to lunch?" "No, I urged her to have something sent up to her room." "Oh yes, she'll have something in her room?" "Yes, then she'll feel better later; she'll be down to dinner." "Oh, she'll be down to dinner?" "Yes, I thought if she'd eat something light now, in her room, instead of coming down, she'll feel better." "But she'll be coming down to dinner?" "Oh yes, she'll be down to dinner."

These people will lose the war, I thought. And then knew that of course they wouldn't.

My birthday was November 24. Georgette and I greeted each other with the same phrase—"Thank you for your existence." We drank toasts in Quinquina and Monique made a *grand déjeuner*—roast veal, applesauce, purée of chestnuts. My present was a small bottle of Tabac Blond wrapped in a cluster of honeysuckle and mimosa.

At six o'clock the BBC played our Rachmaninoff Concerto, as if to order. "Ah," Georgette said, "if one could write a book like music. I don't mean to compose one's thought as a musician develops his theme, but to compose and impose magic."

By the end of November Georgette was less well again—perhaps the sea air in Hendaye was too strong for her. I began looking for a house farther inland, and found one in Biriatou, a village six kilometres away.

We moved. Ten trips in the car, four days to transform the house. I considered this no effort at all.

But within a few days Georgette was seriously ill. For sixteen consecutive hours I walked about, ministering. At three in the morning, when the crisis was over, I was so tired that I could no longer stand, or move. I went into the dark kitchen, turned on the little lamp, sat down at the table and ate a chicken wing, with bread and butter, and drank a glass of wine in the silence of the night. I shall never forget how it tasted; or how, after too-great exertion, you enter a different world—a wider place where sound is more sonorous. The night roared in my ears. I went toward the haven of my room and had a real experience: that of entering into the organized peace and order of a room of one's own—a composition, like a strain of music. As I staggered through the door, in the dark, a street lamp shone through the curtains with the effect of moonlight. I sat down and felt my nervous system take on again its own rhythm, as my eyes picked out every object—the bed following the lines of two walls, the little *guéridon* with its lamp, the long line of my work table and the perfect angle in the position of the armchair. Some people say that objects arranged in a design have no effect, healing or otherwise, on their organisms. I don't understand them.

. . . The illness was caused by carbonic acid fumes escaping from the kitchen stove into the connecting chimney of Georgette's room. So we decided to move back to Hendaye.

These two movings comprised twenty trips in the car; the construction of a new environment, then its destruction; the reconstruction of a former environment which had been "destroyed" but, fortunately, not rented; to say nothing of the persuasions brought to bear upon a bewildered landlady. Again I was unaware of effort.

And after the effort of reconstruction, with improvements, of the Villa Victor Marie, I remember sitting on the terrace until darkness came, listening to the cadence of the sea. Any environment becomes beautiful as night falls and the first star appears. I realized how my feeling about the sea had changed since I was young. Then I liked it more than mountains; now I prefered the peace of mountains. The sea to me now was active, mountains passive, and I preferred passivity as a background for my too-active life. The truth, of course, was exactly the opposite: I, as a completely passive unit, no longer wanted the activity of the sea but felt more comfortable beside mountains, which also sit. A terrible picture—I tried not to look at it. Was there any real activity in my life—in the Gurdjieff sense? Almost none. And perhaps I meant to go on this way? Does anyone ever really change? Not in your nature, Gurdjieff said. But in other ways. At least I now understood something about the other ways.

We kept trying not to founder in war emotions, but every night I sat hypnotized before the radio. The BBC was as clear in my room as if I had been in London. Strange phenomenon . . . the world-psyche tuned in to nine-o'clock news.

Two gentle little old maids living in our street asked us to tea—Mlles. Rivale and Crepet (names for Anatole France). Forty-five years ago they had lived in Bordeaux, had heard Georgette sing "Thaïs," "Carmen," "Fidelio" at the Opéra; now they had been lying in wait for her. The world is full of romantic people, we thought. These two old gentlewomen—one so timid that she laughed every time she spoke and murmured aloud an advance notice of every gesture ("I'd better put on the kettle for tea, huh, huh, huh")—had lived with an inner excitement comparable to our own. They were fascinated by Georgette, who had regained all her beauty; her eyes had never been

192

more brilliant (she was now seventy). "I feel today as when very young," she said, "when I used to say *'Aujourd-'hui je fais du soleil.'*" "You mustn't talk like that," her nurse said. Why, instead, didn't she say "What a wonderful picture to have thought of?" It explains a gift—probably related to one's batteries of personal magnetism.

Georgette read her chapter, "A Well of Water," to the eager old ladies and they asked if they might come and talk with her, and hear more of Gurdjieff.

A letter . . . wounding to read, after so many years of effort on my part to explain the scope of Gurdjieff's teaching.

It rambled on: "I can naturally follow in some measure his intention, his aim. There is a definite relationship to Christianity—that I do realize. I believe in Gurdjieff's surgery, but I want a clean operation. His knife for purging is a dirty instrument and inevitably it leaves some of the virus in the wounds. I do not doubt that Gurdjieff meets many of the needs of those who follow him, but he cannot forgive sin or give peace—only God can redeem man by His power of love."

It would do no good if I should ask, "But why should God do it all?" Gurdjieff won't let you "sit" in the religious trance, hoping for redemption—it's psychopathic. If the religious impulse doesn't exist in you, he cannot work with you; if it is latent he draws it out, finds how much you have, allows you to bask in it for a while, then helps you to understand the impulse and develop it. "Just as I am, without one plea" is not enough. Find out what you are *not*, and do something about it. The only clean knife I know.

From New York came a warning that all Americans must leave France or risk being put into "friendly" concentration camps. My heart stopped. We could never face separation. I found myself thinking of our two revolvers, still hidden safely in the car.

The American Consulate in Bordeaux announced that if I meant to stay on in France, against their advice, I must have my passport validated. We stayed overnight in Bordeaux and walked under the *galeries* of the Opéra, where Georgette used to promenade in her trailing gowns, carrying Maeterlinck's letters in her purse which, otherwise, she might have lost. It was with this ecstasy of the written word that she began her dream of life. That dream died but the ecstasy never died. *Then* she stepped out upon a stage with a walk of triumph; *now* she barely had the strength to stroll under the arcades; then she was young, beautiful and full of fire; now she was . . . young, beautiful and full of fire.

I took some snapshots. Jane wrote from London: "Georgette looks so renewed, assured, untouched." "She can't be really ill," we kept telling ourselves.

One night she talked about the radiance that resides in the *format* of certain people. Thinking back to those days of opera in Bordeaux, Paris and Bruxelles,—"the too-much that is in me," she called it. Sylvain, the critic, and his wife used to sit in a box night after night and watch her on the stage. "Why?" she asked him in an interview. "I don't know," he said, "I don't know what it is you have. My wife feels the same way—there is something we don't understand." "But I do," Georgette said, "I know what it is. It's *la chose de vie*. It's not merely a question of art; even people completely insensitive to art respond to this 'thing of life.' "

I knew what she meant—the lack of it is what disconcerts you in the life of people. Georgette added, "But there is always three-quarters of me in a cage. It tries to get out—it is the too-much that doesn't find an outlet. I was twenty in those days and now, fifty years later, it is the same—I have never found enough outlets for *la chose de vie*."

. . . Perhaps that capacity "to make sun."

Mid-December, and we almost had a visitor. But we refused—we couldn't afford a temperamental guest. As Georgette said, "Temperament is the soil I like best in people, but the intelligence must be of equal force—otherwise *c'est un désastre*." This particular temperament had innumerable friends, acquaintances, social relations— why did she turn to us, I asked, when our lives and aims were at such opposite poles? Georgette said, "We seem like friends to her; she really has no friends. *Les gens à relations n'ont pas d'amis*."

I never stop wondering how "sensitive" people can be so insensitive to their own atmosphere—to the ambience they carry with them. It is difficult to explain to a person of temperament, of too-strong personality, exactly what you object to in her behavior. You can't say, "I just don't want you to come into a room as you do, bringing too much with you." Such people always carry with them that definite personal-authority bang that disrupts the atmosphere already existing in a room. For them everything must pass through, and be colored by, the color of their personality. But one gets so weary of "personality." It always operates through the particular quirk your self-love has built up—what Gurdjieff calls your "manifestations." You finally come to realize how redundant are all the manifestations you present to him. The picture makes you a little sick.

The war stood still. France took no precautions about rationing. We still had enough gas for the car. The only restrictions on food were two meatless days a week. Chickens were plentiful and cost only twenty-eight francs.

But Georgette couldn't eat or sleep. On certain days her eyes were set in deep shadows; on others a flame burned the shadows away. We began to reckon in terms of spirit alone.

Death was still only a word. But we began to be conscious of a presence: doom.

And then Christmas came. We shut ourselves more closely into our world, we composed a Christmas of thanksgiving for all that we had; for we still had all things—all that one ever needs or longs for—except one: the promise of continuation. We assembled all the symbols of the living earth—"*des fruits, des fleurs, des feuilles et des branches"*; we found a blue Christmas tree and covered it with vermillion flowers; we made a *fête* of scents— pinecones and incense and sealing-wax; we lighted long candles and ate a feast in their wavering light. An enchantment was upon us. I knew it would have been less had we been happy people in an assured world. In the afternoon we walked on the beach, watched the waves run along the sand, rush at us and recede. We were very gay. Under all our spoken words of love and hope there ran, for me, the deepest of the themes of love: I will find some way of infinite care, I will keep you from all harm.

For New Year's we decided to read again all the notes we had taken during our experience with Gurdjieff, beginning in 1924—fragments from lectures, re-formulations from his manuscript made by Orage, or Jane. What had been the first words that convinced us we were hearing something different from all that we had found in all the books, in all the cults? What great statements had most impressed us in the first year?

I said, "To begin with, I remember my impression when I heard this: 'The universe is an intelligent scheme (plan, idea) and is therefore intelligible. The Gurdjieff ideas are a pattern of thinking—a great thinking-machine. Any question the mind of man can put has been answered. At the base of things there is not just a mystery. The natures of things lie together in harmony. The real world is the evolution of an idea.' "

Georgette said, "I shall never forget my emotion when I first heard these words: 'Man's obligation is to cooperate with the laws which operate the universe. The realization of the working of certain laws is the kingdom of heaven.' "

"Yes," Monique said, "and do you remember what followed that? 'The obligation goes with the fact that man has a unique place. But the awareness of his place is not a gift of nature. No man by *wishing*, or by taking thought, can do anything about his development. He must do something unique. The Gurdjieff method offers this unique activity.' "

"And this," Georgette said. " 'Since we have no technique for development, our life is like a dream. In dreams we don't choose or invent events. Our life is like that. And we can't voluntarily wake from this dream. One wakes, or develops, only if the dream becomes unbearable, or if someone shakes us awake.' "

I said: "Remember this?: the Gurdjieff vocabulary is as precise as that of any other science. All the terms used in the Bible were once precise scientific terms."

Georgette said, "One of my great days at the Prieuré was when I first heard that the octave was originally a formula to explain cosmological truths—only later was it used musically."

"I remember the definition of the octave," Monique said. " 'A mathematical formula in respect of sound, through which all creation (physical and psychical) must pass, upward and downward, in the phenomenal changes of nature.' "

"I remember another definition," I said. " 'Time is only the exhaustion of the means to renew ourselves.'
198

That made me really think. And then what followed: 'By conscious thoughts, emotions, acts, we feed ourselves. God, when He made the universe, made self-feeding.' "

"Consciousness" . . . Georgette said. "I remember this: 'A state of consciousness has a place (relative position) in the cosmos. The Sermon on the Mount—a high state of consciousness.' "

I said, "One of Gurdjieff's definitions that always moves me most is this one: 'Knowledge and Understanding are quite different. Only understanding can lead to Being, whereas knowledge is only a passing presence in it. . . . One must *strive* to understand. This alone can lead to our Lord God, and in order to understand the phenomena of Nature according to Law, one must first of all consciously perceive and assimilate a mass of information concerning objective truth and the events which really took place on the earth in the past; and secondly, one must be the bearer of all kinds of experiencings personally experienced.' "

January 6.

We talked of freedom . . .

I answered a letter in a phrase: "I don't have the ordinary thoughts you speak of."

. . . Among a thousand freedoms I could name, one of the most valued is this one: never to be accused of motives you haven't got. These motives always belong to the people who attribute them to you—and, as Georgette said, "They always present you with small motives, never great ones."

We talked about our mutual passion for "understanding"—for perfected human communication . . . in other words, what Georgette called "*l'entente*." She decided to write a chapter about it for her book. I knew what I would write: Give me understanding or give me death.

Georgette wrote this:

L'Entente (The Art of Communication)

Understanding is not the product of dreams. It does not accompany young love with its roses, its frailty, its empty spaces, its ends and its end. My search for it was long and tireless . . . Later I saw why it is not easy to come upon. I had hoped to match myself with another's existence when I, myself, did not yet exist.

At twenty I confused understanding with love . . . But the understanding that comes from being in love is only a chemical understanding. When it ends, it leaves behind it only sweetness or pain.

Understanding is a sort of love that does not end, because it desires the existence of the loved one as much as its own. I believe it is the only human bond that is not content simply to feed upon its own emotion. It rejects all that can be accepted only if one's eyes are closed, and all that is "impure." In understanding, to lie would be senseless; there are no permissions to be accorded, no commandments to be imposed. Understanding is above tolerance and tests. It is a bond which would not be if it were not perfect.

One cannot have understanding without a double knowledge —one must know oneself and the other person . . . I know, for example, that I will never be understood by the "material-world" category. I have nothing in common with those solid friendships which maintain themselves on the every-day plane I abhor. They have something a little *concierge* about them. Such friends become like two business associates—their strength is doubled but they are not concerned with the quality of their relationship. Of what value is a friendship which does not help you to understand more of yourself, of the other, and of all others?

My first perfect understanding—a pure rapture—was with a poet. A poet never says "It is impossible" or "It is incredible"—he carries within himself a belief in stars, he turns his imagination upon all the earth, the dark of his night is as clear as the light of his day. . . . Above all, I lived in the ecstasy of being understood. For the first time someone believed in the fervent substance of my own created world.

I can name any number of tendencies which preclude a relationship of understanding. A vice can prevent it—especially a vice like avarice or indelicacy; a too-spherical egoism, a slackening of *élan*, an aging of the cells, a lack of good faith, a lack of distinction, or a lack of that serious lightness which is so rewarding in human relationships. Heavy human vibrations can prevent it; an empty agitated mind; a ponderous frivolity; people who splash on entering a room as if they were diving; people of sonorous authority whose words clatter like hail against a window; intelligent people whose vibrations are impressive but who never speak a word of truth—they approach everything so indirectly that one wonders how they manage to get through a doorway; talkers with impetuous emanations who push aside everything in their path to make way for their monologues; people who have no presence at all—their emanations have been clipped off close to their bodies, like shorn sheep; the chronometer people who regulate everything and everyone; and those who strike, who bite, who scratch, who sting, who lie, who eject their venom wherever their anger falls, while their emanations claw and their mouths are pulled into a bitter twist . . .

When I was very young I wrote in my diary: "Great ideas are treated like *objets d'étagère*, they are not used. I shall use them." I have kept my word. The great concept contained in "understanding" is what I have always sought, what I have tried to be worthy of, what I have finally found—in the benediction of a true com-

munication with another human being. Ah, if we could only continue to live it for a thousand years!

On the night of January 7 the BBC gave a concert.
I was unprepared for it, I had just opened my windows,
turned off my light, except for the faint gleam from the
radio for the midnight news. Instead of news I heard a
woman's voice singing something I didn't know, in a way
singers never sing. The speaker announced that Madame
someone whose name I couldn't catch would sing something whose title I couldn't hear. It was almost coloratura
soprano but handled differently, with luxury, as if the
voice had all the time in the world to establish a spell of
music. Then the announcer said, "Strauss's 'Morgen.' " The
orchestra took the opening measures more slowly than they
are ever played, and then that voice began to lead the
orchestra and the song through an evocation of a lost
world—a world where musicians had time to feel and
record their emotions about the beginning of day . . .
a whole life that was no longer taking place on a planet
at war. There is nothing more shattering than a too-slow
tempo, but this was so slow that the song became an im-
provisation—as the composer must first have heard it in
his mind. I imagined the singer conducting the orchestra
to give her voice the space in which to create, pianissimo,
this sad ecstasy: morning music sung at night, full of
tears. There was silence when she had finished—even the
announcer sounded too moved to say her name clearly.
So I have never known who it was.

Georgette finished her book on January 26—except for the Gurdjieff part, which she knew would need months of "evocative" editing. I wondered if any American publisher would ever take it. What would I say to a publisher who asked what it was about? Good heavens. I might say: how wonderful, how unbelievable, that anyone should have been able to give such expression to such thoughts—such exquisite expression, like her singing. I would say, "This book is a formulation of a great kind of life. I don't know whether the world cares to read about such life, but please publish the book anyway and you will find that it does." Bravo!—that would certainly convince him.

In February we left for Cannes where friends had found us a flat. More realistic than we, they knew that the moment would come when we must deal with pain, and doctors.

The flat was in Le Cannet, three kilometres above Cannes. We arrived there on the tenth of February, 1940, and felt, once again, that we had entered a dream. Our balcony looked over the Mediterranean; our windows looked over the Place Bellevue where peasants came in the morning with narcissus, daffodils and jonquils and arranged them on tables under the plane trees; where old women and young girls came with their pitchers to the fountain. There was a little café with chairs on the street, a *mercerie*, a *boucherie* with a red and white awning, an *épicerie* full of formal vegetables and wine bottles, a *pharmacie* for all our needs. We had a telephone and there was a good doctor three blocks away. The flat was full of pale Provençal bowls to hold the narcissus; the windows were filled with branches of plane trees, church chimes and, later in the spring, the smell of orange blossoms.

For four months we lived in this arcadia. Georgette bloomed, and my memories are of such breathless hope and conviction that they identify only with the lengthening days of spring and the eternal renewal of life. We went into the country with baskets of bread and wine, patés and pastries, cheese, fruits and coffee and spread them out under olive trees. Monique walked among the wild hyacinths, gathering bouquets; Georgette sat under a nettle tree; the war was far away, the Midi sun passed slowly across the sky, the olive trees turned to silver mist.

But one day we went to see a doctor in Nice. He said, "She can't possibly live more than six months." We didn't believe him. We were right. She lived eighteen months more.

FLIGHT INTO NOWHERE

Before the end of May it was obvious that Italy was coming into the war, and in Cannes people talked of bombings. We decided to flee—back toward Spain and Portugal . . . a journey of eight hundred kilometres, but we could still get all the gas we needed. My garage man filled up the tank—107 litres—and gave me ten extra five-litre cans. We left at five o'clock in the afternoon, on May 31, and were in Brignolles by seven. The next day several bombs fell in Cannes and a child was killed not far from where we lived. We heard that people were already leaving Nice and other coast towns for the center of France, but we met no one on the roads.

The Château Tivoli in Brignolles was one of my favorite hotels because of its long arched galleries, its poplars and cypresses and nightingales, its diningroom with a raised platform at the end where a log fire was always burning, even in May; it was a fire superior to others, with logs placed so that they never smouldered but burned brightly to the end.

That night's dinner was the beginning of a series that now have a special climate for me—war dinners. There was a quality of false excitement about them that you couldn't help enjoying. You went into a diningroom, tired from driving, worn by the obsession of war approaching, whatever you did, wherever you fled—perhaps you had fled to the very place where it would catch up with you. But you decided to forget this menace for one night, to dine once more in peace, enjoy fine French food as never before, relax under the slow smooth wine. I sat for a long time by the fire, wondering if we couldn't arrange to stay on in this calm place instead of worrying about getting to America. Finally I went to my room and looked out at the Provençal night. There were the cypress trees where they had always been, standing in fields whitened by the moon; and one of the Brignolles nightingales was singing in the woods.

In the morning I asked to keep our rooms for a week, but was told that all rooms had been reserved by people telephoning from Riviera hotels within the last few days. We had beaten them by one night. From this moment my personal attitude toward the war became a race to beat events, to keep Georgette out of the range of refugees and bombs.

I went to the garage and drove the car around to the front door. As I sat there, planning, a soldier came in through the outer gates and told me to go back into the hotel. I obeyed without understanding, and then I heard a faint noise—not at all as I had imagined air-raid sirens would sound in a crisis. No attack followed. Georgette was in her bath and heard nothing at all.

Before we started off a car drove in from the direction of Aix-en-Provençe. A woman got out and warned us that if we were going that way we would find no hotel rooms. "The roads around Montpellier and all the other towns in that region are full of people coming in from all directions; they don't know where they're going, they're waiting for news."

We set out on the route we had planned—Arles, Montpellier, Toulouse, Auch, Condon, Langon, Bordeaux —and found no people at all on the roads—which didn't surprise me: I never believe in the predictions of others. After we passed Toulouse the landscape became park and garden country, fresh and elegant, any part of which we should have liked to stay in forever. After Auch we drove into a village called Castelverduzan and stopped before an inn which, at a glance, could be recognized as a landmark. The proprietor served our lunch in a garden, under an avenue of trees where Henri IV and his court used to stroll. Again we debated whether we should settle down here for the duration and mind our own business, instead of being manipulated by events; but again we realized that doctors, medicines and X-ray machines were now our business. We talked with a group of Belgian refugees sitting in the garden, committed to doing nothing; they were very bored because they had left Bruxelles and couldn't get back.

By five o'clock we were in Bordeaux at the American Consulate, which was overflowing with desperate people. The *S. S. Washington* was scheduled to sail on the eighth of June and visas could be had for Georgette and me, but none for Monique, since Belgium no longer had the status of a nation—it was now considered merely a place that had been overrun by the Germans. There was no way (that I knew of) to influence the consul's decision, and we couldn't leave Monique behind. We drove to the hotel, holding our despair in check, knowing that we must face it during the night, though we would only decide again what we had immediately decided.

The Royal Gascogne had no rooms, people were reserving armchairs for the night in the foyer and halls. Finally the management offered a solution—two rooms in a *maison de passe* where we slept in a setting of red plush and, to my surprise, an amazing amount of good literature.

The next day I spent nine hours getting our *permis de circulation* from French officials who had become more self-important and more enamoured of red-tape than ever, now that France was in danger. By evening we were equipped with enough papers to leave Bordeaux and we set off vaguely in the direction of Bayonne—near enough to Hendaye and Spain to allow us to sail as soon as Belgium had again become a nation.

Twenty-five kilometres south of Bordeaux we drove into a village called Saucats. The inn had two free rooms on the garden and a bed in a vast bare dance-hall called the *salle des roses*, where I might sleep "if I wasn't afraid." Though it was on the ground floor and open to village marauders, I decided that I wasn't afraid. I put our two revolvers (now supposed to be turned in to the government) under my pillow. We dined in the dark garden, drank white wine in candlelight, and had a night of silence, sleep and forgetfulness.

There was peace in this village, no lack of food, no refugee traffic on the roads, and we decided to stay a week. But on the third day people passed through in cars, carrying rumors of the beginning of that mass flight from Paris which was soon to block all the roads. So we went on to Bayonne and found rooms in the Grand Hotel. People were streaming in, chairs in the lounge were offered as beds to the tired crowds and everyone gathered around the radio, which gave out almost no news. People were still hopeful, no one suspected how badly the war was going for France.

The garage where I put the car looked like a tenement backyard—nearly every car had a mattress fastened over the top and housewives had opened all their baggage, washed clothes and hung them up to dry on clothes lines, so that you couldn't see to drive through them.

It was too late for dinner in the hotel and we went in search of a restaurant. Reynaud was to talk at nine-thirty and the café radio tuned in. But no one listened. Soldiers who strolled in for coffee, and many young men of conscription age without uniforms, talked so loudly through the speech that we couldn't hear. When I asked the waitress what Reynaud was saying she answered, "Oh, just something about the war." It was his "good news" speech, inserted between the one he had made on King Leopold and a third, which was to be his piteous appeal to Roosevelt for clouds of planes.

After the third speech everyone became tense and

209

serious about the war. The hotel clientèle sat hour after hour before the radio, which now gave out no news at all; announcers merely kept repeating, "There is no answer yet from Roosevelt." Defeat, capitulation, surrender, armistice, were terms still undreamed of.

When the Germans began marching toward Paris no announcement was made; I heard the news from London —we were the only people in the hotel whose radio had short waves. Finally, as the French radio kept up its silence, the BBC announced that the Germans were nearing Paris, that it might be proclaimed an open city.

The next few days were days of anguish over Paris. But they were something more personal too—they were days of physical fear. The Germans bombed Bordeaux and a hundred people were killed in the Place de la Comédie, where we had sat, waiting for permits, only a few days before. For the first time I began to realize what, until now, had been beyond my imagination—the fact of a bomb killing or maiming the person you love. What ought we to do? No one knew.

I watched people meeting in the lobby, families finding each other again after being separated on the roads. Strangers wept as they watched the reunited families weeping. A car drew up outside, under the chestnut trees. Virgil Thomson got out and came into the hotel with some friends. He was calm and somehow comforting, but he too said he didn't know what to do, except to try for a boat to New York.

Then it was said that Bayonne might be bombed any night. We kept this rumor from Georgette, but all night I sat in my room, in bed, experiencing fear. People had always told me how their bodies acted under extreme fear —icy hands, twitching muscles, failing knees. I had never had these reactions, I knew only the tenseness of an accelerated heartbeat. But on this night, for the first time, I trembled in every muscle as waves of fear swept over me. All the minutes of the night, as I sat rigidly waiting for the first sound of sirens, I trembled and shook, even my bed shook. My thoughts were divided between curiosity about my physical helplessness and astonishment that I hadn't already packed a bag with essentials that we could carry to the cellar in case of bombing. I also thought a great deal about the human body as a marvelous machine, and how it had not been designed as a target for steel bombs. Only when daylight came did I find the strength to get out of bed and rush around the room packing a bag. From this moment it was always within reach, day and night.

We entered the race for *visas de sortie* at the Préfecture. The crowd was so dense there, hour after hour, that it seemed never to move. A thunderstorm burst over us as we stood under the *galeries* and I saw a boy sitting on a bicycle knocked off by a bolt that seemed to set him on fire. He lay on the ground a moment, as if destroyed, then got up as if nothing had happened. No one paid any attention.

We got no visas. Our passports had been sent off to Bordeaux, with the necessary request papers; then officially lost. It was a month before they were found.

The Germans entered Paris, but the French in our

hotel didn't suffer about it as we did. They seemed mainly to be relieved that Paris wouldn't be bombed. For that matter, though it made me feel vaguely unpatriotic, I remember my own relief.

But on the day of the German entrée into Paris Dr. Thierry de Martel killed himself.

He told his closest friend: "I am over sixty, I expect nothing more from life, and I don't want to see the Germans march down the Champs Elysees."

He had already confided this to our ambassador, William Bullitt, who had nevertheless persuaded him to "remain at his post." The next day Martel sent him the following message:

"*Je vous ai fait la promesse de ne pas quitter Paris. Je ne vous ai pas dit si je resterais à Paris vivant or mort. En y restant vivant, c'est un chèque barré que je remets à nos adversaires. Si j'y reste mort, c'est un cheque sans provision. Adieu.*" *

He gave himself a *piqure* of strychnine.

Monique and I took turns sitting up all night outside the Portuguese Consulate to get our visas for that country, without which no Spanish transit visas would be issued. We never got them. Only a few English people were successful and they rushed away in a truck, leaving handsome motor cars abandoned in the streets.

---

* "I promised you not to leave Paris. I didn't say whether I would remain there dead or alive. If I remain alive I represent, for our adversaries, a certified check. Dead, I am a check marked 'no funds.' Farewell."

. . . June 16, and the radio announced that Marshal Pétain would speak. We all gathered again in the hotel salon. We waited most of the night and nothing happened. The next morning on the radio we heard a weary voice— not at all firm, as I have since read, but old, unemotional, wavering—explain that France had asked for an armistice. The translations of this speech have been inadequate; its style was the only thing you listened to—it was the purest classicism. For the next two years Pétain never spoke without giving me the impression that he had lifted his syntax straight out of St. Just.

After the armistice France became very moral. I could no longer appear in slacks on the street without attracting a crowd of enraged Frenchmen; the ones who had most enjoyed American ways and freedom now declared that it was America that had caused France's downfall. They yelled epithets at me as I walked the block from the garage to the hotel, until I felt that a French revolution was forming behind me. For once I had to keep silent and reach the hotel quickly without appearing to hurry.

Refugees from Paris began to pour into Bayonne and they behaved like the French we had always loved, with unbelievable spirit and courage. I talked with one old woman who had walked from Paris to Orléans, carrying two enormous suitcases—it was impossible but she had done it. In our small restaurant one day there appeared a man, his wife, a boy of eight and a wheelbarrow. They had taken a train out of Paris but had been put off somewhere along the road and had walked more than 400 kilometres, pushing their household goods in the wheelbarrow, sleeping in fields.

Then we heard that the Germans were entering Bayonne.

We didn't look at them, but we couldn't help seeing them. They were all tall and thin, except one, and the first thing they did was to invade the chocolate shops under the arcades. Their uniforms were far superior, in cloth, color and cut, to the French; they had metal hooks around the waist to hold their belts, and the hooks were placed low enough to give every man a long line from shoulder to waist. As they walked in groups through the streets I couldn't help watching the beauty of their rhythm. They all had it—a long legato stride. And they drove their cars differently from any Frenchman; you could always distinguish a German foot on the accelerator by the quick force and dash of the sound.

The town began to smell like an army—a dull, heavy unaired smell. I lunched under the arcades wherever I saw Germans and Frenchmen in groups, and listened to them trying to talk to each other. Many Frenchmen were sympathetic to the conquerors, especially those who were most ashamed of themselves. When they couldn't understand each other in words they used pantomime—a Frenchman would say "Daladier" or "Reynaud" and then make a gesture of slashing his throat; the German would grin and say "*Ja, ja.*"

A young French girl complained to a German officer that one of his soldiers had pushed against her in the street. The officer called the soldier, made him kneel down on the sidewalk and ask the girl's pardon; then he slashed him twice across the face with his stick so brutally that every Frenchman on the street gasped.

Every day in our restaurant a pretty French prostitute sat at a table surrounded by young Germans who talked with the help of pocket dictionaries. The youngest soldier took her under his protection and always sat with his arm around her. He was downy-cheeked and looked as quietly romantic as a young Robert Schumann. The girl's lip-rouge shocked him and every day he tried to explain to her, with gestures, that no nice girl used rouge on her cheeks or lips. He made no progress with her looks, but obviously with her heart, for within a few days his comrades were drinking to their betrothal.

One morning I came in from shopping, with two large bags, and the elevator boy explained that I would have to walk upstairs—the Germans had stopped the elevators to get a clear reception of a Hitler speech. This made me angry and I walked into the salon in a daring mood, not caring what might happen, interested only in protesting my rights and perhaps breaking up the speech. Twenty officers were seated around the radio trying to hear Hitler. I went up to the most important-looking one and complained in French that I couldn't walk up four flights of stairs with two heavy bags. Four or five of the Germans got up, bowed, made polite gestures, explained in good French that their Fuehrer was speaking. I talked as long and as loudly as possible, rivaling their Fuehrer's voice, but they remained mild and increasingly polite. I realized that even if they missed the speech they wouldn't behave unkindly to me, so there was nothing to do but walk away, feeling deflated and rather like a boor.

At last we received substitutes for our lost passports, and then exit visas to leave Bayonne. We were eager to get out of the occupied zone, but I was nervous as we approached the line of demarcation, fearing that our papers might be found insufficient.

We came to the boundary, just outside Orthez, and I saw a single soldier standing guard. He stopped us and then I saw how young he was. He didn't want to look at our papers but at us, and he finally said, with a sympathetic smile, "Cinema stars?" I was about to say, "No, writers," but realized that he might ask "What do you write?" So I said, also with a sympathetic smile, "Yes, cinema stars." He waved to us as we went on.

It was now August and the gas allowance was still high enough for us to reach the center of France. We went to a family château in St. Pardoux-la-Choisille, Corrèze, but finding it full of people stayed at a nearby inn set in pine forests, within sound of a waterfall. Here we lived for a month in a trance of peace. Georgette discovered a place in the woods where the smell of pine was concentrated to an elixir. We called it *"la salle verte"* and spent our afternoons there, consciously breathing enough pine air to compensate Georgette for not always having lived under pine trees, as she would have wished.

But she was failing now . . . It wasn't visible in her

face, but in her walk, her gestures. We looked on, helpless. One fact sustained us: she had no pain.

. . . There was a curving stone wall and a great tree. One night at midnight Georgette and I sat there for an hour— one of those unforgettable hours that remain with you to be relived forever. There was deep silence in the hills, though the waterfall was tinkling in the distance. We didn't speak, but our thoughts were so strong that each could hear the other's. I knew that we were both remembering the days of our life, days on an earth that we had known so many years together, and so loved; I knew that we were saying an advance farewell to all this life and love, a farewell to each other that perhaps we could never say in words. The moon was bright in the silence—"the incomparable moon," I said to myself; not a poetic adjective, I thought, but an exact one, since the moon is the only thing of its kind. I saw its incomparable light shining over us, as our life had always shone. Later, when the fact of separation was upon us, we did not speak; and I knew then that Georgette had known we could not, and had said all that she would say in that moonlight without words.

TO DIE WITHOUT DYING

By September 1940 I knew that we would never get to America. We went back to Le Cannet, in the unoccupied zone, praying that it would remain free until the war had been won.

Our flat had been rented, but high up in the hills I found a little box of a house hanging among olive trees, with red roses running through their branches. It had only three rooms—two small bedrooms and underneath them, like a Swiss chalet, a studio-kitchen. "The Chalet Rose" . . . that was its name.

I bought a green table for our suspended garden, a blue parasol, three green basket chairs, and put them among the pink and white flowers. At noon we drank our wine there and watched the Mediterranean shining below us; late at night I sat there and watched the sky overflow with stars. Night after night Orion shone in Georgette's window.

October passed; November, December—another Chrismas like a gift of time, with friends and a borrowed cat named Moutzie. January came . . . 1941. Georgette's birthday was February 8, but before that day her left hand had begun to swell.

Day by day the swelling increased, day by day we watched its monstrous progress. By April her whole arm had outgrown human proportions. *"Je ne suis pas malade du tout,"* she assured us, *"j'ai simplement eu une accident —comme un bras cassé."* She continued her plans for New York, where she would sing her memorable songs. I realized that it was now too late even to record these songs, with all their art and incomparable diction. I don't know why I didn't find some way for it to be done, but the truth is that I thought only of ways to conceal our grief from Georgette. Two years before she had begun a series of recordings: Reynaldo Hahn's little masterpieces, Duparc, Ravel, Debussy—scenes from *Pélleas* in which she sang the two voices; but she hadn't been satisfied with the first samples and had fallen ill before she could make others. Now she sang these songs softly to herself before sleeping, or to us as twilight closed the days.

Dr. Gros (head of the American Hospital in Paris) wrote that there was nothing to do but to continue X-rays; he hadn't much faith that they would help—the operation had been done so late. "The important thing is what you are doing—keeping her happy, keeping her at her book, keeping up her faith that she is getting better."

But those were the easy efforts. What obsessed me was that there must be something else, something no one yet knew, something that would be discovered—perhaps in

America; some new cure. A miracle must be produced. But where was the scientist who would make the discovery? when would we hear of him, how could we get to him? where find the money, how get visas during a war?

I could only go on planning "happiness," interest, beauty, the life of art . . . and talking of the ideas of Gurdjieff.

It was now twelve months since the doctor in Nice had given Georgette only six more to live. Monique and I entered into a paralysis of identification, always thinking, "This may be our last year." It became super-identification —I found myself saying "I may never see trees again." Even when we were alone, we no longer talked of Georgette's extremis. We had become so used to fostering an illusion that we kept it up even when she slept and we were free to face reality.

All the doctors said that she couldn't support another operation. Even if they should amputate her arm, the horror would reappear somewhere else. I kept feeling that I was looking at the earth for the last times, that I must absorb all of it I could before going away. Georgette gave no sign of ever having such thoughts. Her faith that she would be cured was as indestructible as her faith in the recurrence of spring.

One day I went to Nice and came back in the evening. I hurried up the 117 steps, I opened the door to Georgette's room, I looked once again at her luminous face, listened again to her dazzling greeting, I thought "There is more life in your presence than in the composite presence of a thousand people I have seen today in the streets of Nice." And I remembered a poem she had written not long ago:

I dreamed I was a fountain,
A well, an ever-springing stream . . .

That night I sat in our triangle of garden, under radiant stars, and tried to express, once again, what I had felt all these years about this flowing presence. Life as against non-life—the phrase kept recurring. A senseless phrase unless I could define non-life. Ah, but I could . . .

Non-life to me is all that does not stir, rise, mount, ring, resound, accrete. It is the presence opposite you that remains inert when you are breathless, that remains un-moved when you are overwhelmed; the presence in which nothing arrives; the presence that leads you to nothing and considers it something; that solicits your interest only after the subject has been betrayed, or the object denied; when all that is rich in substance has been drained away, when the talk has been by-passed and the idea reduced. It is the presence that puts you in prison and keeps you there with-out effort, since you cease to exist the moment it speaks. It is the theme that is never allowed to develop, the orchestra-tion that is never listened to. It is the enthusiasm that is labeled naïve, the originality that goes unrecognized. It is the lyrical always turned into the practical, the political always preferred to the psychological. It is the dead hand that demands to function, the empty space that insists it is full, the uncontributing that *must* contribute, the uncharm-ing that must thrive and flourish, the limited that must limit and define, impose, establish and judge. I know you all, I fear you all—you would starve me to death. I see myself running in frenzied circles in search of meat and drink.

A great specialist from Paris got through from the occupied zone and came to see Georgette. Again: "Amputation?" "No." Again: "There is nothing to do. Keep her from suffering." "What will happen?" "It may develop upward into the neck . . . possibly strangulation." I knew enough not to listen to such words. I knew I would know what to do.

Our twenty-eight thousand francs would not last forever and we were now to experience new benedictions of friendship. Help came from several countries—from Belgium, England, America, Cuba—from old and new friends who really convinced us that it is more blessed to give than to receive. I remember the day when Hemingway sent four hundred dollars, "for old times," and how I found a way to change it into francs at seventy to the dollar.

Jane was in London and she and Georgette began a correspondence that was to sustain us through the months to come. Jane neither spoke nor wrote French, and Georgette knew nothing of English except what she had gleaned from rapid American talk; but she was determined to communicate, so she invented a language that would convey her thought. She wrote her letters without asking any help.

Jane to Georgette: I keep it in my mind that only physical things have a beginning and an end, that other things have no beginnings and no end, they remain always. No war can change

223

these things, nor space, nor time, nor distance. Whether you go to America or remain in France, and I remain here, I always say: acts of love, thoughts of love, words of love and understanding, and our efforts to become—these or the results of these things never vary. If we could only understand that it is the same Great Self in all of us; that we are only like beads strung on that Great Self—that we have no self of our own until we become one with *that* self, through work and detachment from our infatuation with the bead that we now are. Dear Georgette, I wish I could be of help. If you have need of my help I also have need to give that help.   *Jane.*

Georgette to Jane: Wonderful Jane, you are so admirable, so courageous—you are alone in the strong life—alone in the large mind—alone in the unique and real sky who is on the earth. You understand me? My english difficulte today—on the paper —and by my mind who is tired. In five night and days I have rote because the charming Cocteau dou a introduction for my book. Then I have seen all the pages with *his* eyes spécial of Cocteau. Certainely we change with the lecteur, like I can only rite in english for you! I am today very far of my body, so tired . . . my dear, I hope to see you very soon. Come on, very soon, quikly. My heart.   *Georgette.*

Jane to Georgette: Dear Georgette—what an amazing woman you are! You finish your book in the midst of physical calamities. You are truly a Phoenix. How I love your letters. I read and reread them and laugh until I cry. Your English always delights me—you make it unbearably funny—a perfect caricature of the spoken word. Sometimes I am forced to howl at your unexpectedness. This is only the outside of course. I am deeply touched that you write me such letters.   *Jane.*

Georgette to Jane: Dear Jane, dear dear Jane, I am crazy, so crazy! but high crazy. Because something arrive today.

Now nécéssary said the dramatic story who was in my head since war . . . First with opération, thing of the earth, I was very very down, terrible down. You understand certainely. A little after, the second stade arrive—she his more spirituelle and disparing because she said me—"Now I have lost Gurdjieff; impossible learn; my times is broken. Finish all the miracles, they are finish." It was so terrible. You imagine this horror. Long times I réméne like this = it was every minute like a poignard in my body. I said—"It is neurasthénie, I am dead before my death." I cannot said, my dear Jane—I was only a machine, I dont know how I have keep my apperence of life. Any unhapiness is nothing before this drama! And today the most wonderfull is come! Margaret make a traduction of a man of Thibet!!—the real signification of the war, signification so great! soudainly I am happy to be in this age—hapiness réal, and large, *so great* for my little humanity. Jane, I see all the things. It is wonderful choice, on another plan. I am aout of my poor personelle tragédy—naow it is only leight, only sun! I love you, dear Jane. Tendresses very large. *Georgette Leblanc.*

Jane to Georgette: Your moving and beautiful formulation of your two states and your experience of enlightenment has been an experience for me too, and again is vivid evidence of your power to contact those higher matters which give us flashes of divinity . . . Your nature, your organism, as Gurdjieff has often said, is particularly responsive to such contacts. So you were made "high crazy" and raised out of those depleting states. I am sure your experience will save you from a return of dark states.

As for your "disparing" over the loss of Gurdjieff, that was imagination. You can never be cut off unless you yourself fail to understand yourself in relation to him. It is never an action, an event, a mistake that cuts one off . . . it is some non-activity in the verb *to be.* You remember in his chapter "Good and Evil" there is much talk about serviceability to God, and lacking this serviceabiliiy the being does not cease to exist but he ceases to be . . . serviceability meaning of value in the design or plan . . . As long as we have this as our highest wish, and make efforts to create a positive neutralizing force in ourselves, we are contributing to absolute good and cannot cease to exist in the mind of God. No more can our contacts with Gurdjieff be cut off. On one side of him you see manifestations of ordinary man, but the other side you must know is always impartial, timeless . . . As long as you have the WISH you can return at any time. I wish I had known you were suffering about this before; but real objective suffering is good, if not unjust to the body.

Give my love to Florence Nightingale Anderson. Bless her heart, I was always afraid I'd be ill and that she would nurse me.   *Jane.*

The awful expected days of pain, and morphine, came. Georgette's fingers and hand and arm were now so swollen that the skin had long since passed what looked like the bursting-point.

After experimenting, the doctor found an effective formula—not pure morphine but a product called Sédol which made Georgette sleep all night without pain. During the day she had only moments of unbearable suffering, and she developed a technique of alleviation: during a crisis we would walk up and down her room, I supporting her arm which was bent at the elbow and remained rigid, and she letting herself cry out. She had two kinds of animal cries—one high and piercing, the other guttural; the first changed the pain from a nerve pain—"like a thousand toothaches," she said—"to a burning pain, easier to bear." Sometimes this lasted for half an hour. I would scream with her, which made her laugh so hard that the pain gradually subsided.

Why the resurgence of her spiritual vitality during this period? Whenever we talked ideas she talked with such intensity that I had to run for a notebook to take down her formulations. I can still see her swiftly translating into French what I read in English from Gurdjieff's book: her right hand was so weak that the writing ran down the page, barely legible—as she seemed barely conscious; but it was always lucid and precisely translated.

Whenever the radio played the *Rosenkavalier* waltzes she came dancing into my room, her heavy arm in a sling, and whirled around in the quick Viennese rhythm, laughing and ecstasying as she had always done. But she had written some poems about death—four of them. They had the simplicity and inspiration of "natural" poetry—essential statements; beautiful, as if she were telling us in advance all the things she wanted us to know for afterward.

Sometimes, as the Sédol was taking effect, she would call me into her room and make a lovely conversation, holding my hand and saying such adorable things about "life" that I could do nothing afterward but cry and cry.

One night in September we couldn't get Sédol and a nurse came up to give a *piqure* of morphine. Its effect was to keep Georgette awake all night, with delirium. In the morning she said, "I don't understand why people enjoy morphine—for me, I become an exile from things." The nurse, who had never seen her before, said to Monique, *"Cette dame a peut-être quarante ans, n'est ce pas?"*

We went down to Cannes to see a film of Tschaikowsky's life, with some of his loveliest songs. Afterward

227

Georgette walked with me along the rue d'Antibes in a transport, climbed the 117 steps, her monster arm hidden under her coat, her breath short but expended upon Tschaikowsky—*"C'est à hurler de beauté!"*

Reynaldo Hahn was conducting at the Casino in Cannes and asked Georgette to be his guest. It took her three hours to dress and arrange her *coiffure de soirée,* with one hand. She went down in the gaz-o-gène bus with our neighbors (I was too worn to go) and Reynaldo took her into his loge and gave her red roses—for *Monna Vanna.* She came back exalted, but the neighbors told me they thought she would faint as they waited an hour, after the performance, for the bus.

She wrote no more poems about death. "There was a moment," she said, "when I feared I might die, but now I know I am getting well. It is simply a matter of patience."

Jane to Georgette: Dear, dear Georgette, there is no way to tell you how sad I am about your arm, and that you are suffering . . . Many bombs have fallen all around our house—the last terrible raid nearly got it—five hundred planes over from 8:45 until 5 A.M. I was fire-watching. It made me feel very grim—the tumult of planes and A.A. guns in the sky—fire rising up to the very center; the balloons were all pink on the underside, looking like giant goldfish in a pale green lake of morning sky. One is not afraid—it is simply death or not death.

When we are in the country the planes go over so low that the slates on our roof rise up and then fall into place again when the suction is past. One night, just before midnight, a plane came whistling over the house, breaking to pieces as it plunged. Part of it fell into one of our fields beside my rooms. Two other parts plunged onward to fall in flames, in fields beyond. It is exciting to watch the body in times like this. That night, before I could think, I stood right up out of bed listening with the whole of me; but no quickened heart, no trembling, only watchfulness—for the "I" and of the "I." Perhaps I should not be writing such things to you when you are in pain, but I think of your interest in all manifestations—perhaps you can feel the resistance and repulsion of danger. It is good to feel unafraid. I am always alone here. I am reading the religions of the world—not the man-made ones, only the divine ones of which Gurdjieff's is one.   *Jane.*

October was a cold month. Food began to be scarce, there was almost nothing that Georgette could eat.

Her inner vitality was waning, she had more pain, her attention began to turn from psychical to physical needs. She was determined not to stay on in Cannes through the winter but planned to go to Algiers. From there, she said, we would go south to the desert—to some oasis where there would be plenty of doctors and medicines. We were to take a cargo boat, we would surely find Sédol in this oasis and all would be well. We said "Yes" to everything.

Sometimes we took a walk in the hills and came back to smell eucalyptus leaves smouldering on the stove. All evening we would talk of our happiness.

Sometimes at ten o'clock, after she had taken her sedative, Monique and I crept back to her door to see if she was sleeping. Once she was lying high on her pillows, singing Honnegger's "Adieu" to herself, very softly. She didn't know we were there. There was a faint smile on her face.

Downstairs I often heard Monique crying in the night. There was nothing I could do.

Jane to Georgette: I think you must feel that this great suffering is "accident" only to the physical body—not "Karma." No one would know from your letters that you were even touched by illness—much less such great suffering. I do not think that I should be able to transform this suffering into consciousness any better than you are doing, and can do. We must all of us, in these times, "wish to be" something that cannot be destroyed. Does the doctor give you something that calms pain but at the same time leaves you not too tired to do a little work on yourself? But doctors know nothing of Spirit—and not much about the physical body; they treat it as something separate from Spirit. "Everything that sways, breathes, opens, closes, lives in Spirit; beyond learning, beyond everything, better than anything" . . . "It is the undying blazing Spirit, that seed of all seeds, wherein lies hidden the world and all its creatures." With Spirit one can conquer everything. Spirit is the *emotional.* "He who knows Spirit knows the foundation. He who knows Spirit as that boundless wise reality, hidden in the heart's cavern, gets all that he wants." Now in this time of suffering perhaps you, with Margaret's help, can put to use that Spirit which made you a little vague in the practical affairs of life—that Spirit you were closer to than all those who, because they knew nothing of Spirit, never understood your speech and ways. God bless you.   *Jane.*

2. It was at this time that a change took place in us. I don't know why or how it happened, but I know that, without speaking of it, we began to feel we were entering a new state, sharing a new attitude. I felt it in the very way we looked at each other.

It was as if overnight, without any need of new knowledge or comfort, we were somehow prepared to take our places in a drama that was to be played out for us and in which we accepted the development and ending as beyond our power to affect. It was like placing our faith in a force that would not betray us, even though it was to lead to death. This is no phenomenon, I suppose; it must be the common reaction to a "fate" that announces its strength; but for us to accept a new fate, one beyond our own competence to transform, was a new state. Perhaps we didn't accept it, perhaps what I felt was merely a recognition that we would try to exercise ourselves in irrevocability. I remember reading about a soldier who knew he had reached finality, who spent his last super-moments looking with all his force at a flower in a field. From this time on, I felt, we would move through a super-state. Monique would gather honeysuckle, I would present confident days; together we would lead her close to a garden; with the help of unknown forces we would preserve her.

Our fear of death became quieter. We entered that transition which leads from despair to destiny, from personal grief to impersonal tragedy, and which is like the shift that occurs in art—from stylelessness to form. I knew that our death-in-life was beginning its transmutation into the octave of life-in-death.

On Sunday, October the thirteenth, Georgette decided to go into a *clinique* where, the doctor said, she could have chicken twice a week and vegetables other than rutabagas.

On Monday morning an ambulance stopped before the green door of the Chalet Rose and our neighbors saw Georgette come out of it, smiling. Her long robe, her draped fur coat and her adieux to her friends, who pressed

long-stemmed flowers into her right arm, suggested a prima
donna leaving a triumph rather than a woman of seventy-
two, mortally ill, entering an ambulance. It was a shining
autumn day. Georgette lay quietly holding her flowers,
watching the passing landscape and saying *"C'est trop
beau"* to Monique and me.

The convent-clinic was on the route to La Bocca, by
the sea, and we stayed there among the smiling and silent
nuns for a week. Every night Georgette seemed to fade
away before our eyes; every morning she seemed to find
fresh life. Every morning she read Gurdjieff, and every
night she said the Lord's Prayer—first in French, then in
English. . . .

By the next Sunday she wanted to return to the charm
and comfort of the Chalet Rose. The doctor agreed. On
Monday morning the ambulance waited for us again and
as we were leaving I watched the doctor blunder for the
first time: to Georgette's question about her condition he
was not quick enough; his face showed for a flash his tragic
knowledge, his reassuring smile came a second too late.
Georgette looked at him intently; then her smile sent him
away, reassured. As the door closed behind him her bear-
ing became that of another person—of one who, at last,
knows. To us she merely said, "He thinks I am not better."
But I knew that the power of suggestibility would now
operate against, rather than for, her.

It was another brilliant October day. Again Georgette
watched the landscape; again she said, *"C'est trop beau"*;
but now it was the saddest phrase in the world—sadder
than anything she had ever said. And I did not know it

could be sadder still—as it was, with a change of inflection, a week later.

3. The week to come, in the Chalet Rose, was the last week of Georgette's life.

In her flower-filled room she said to Monique (she would never speak of death to me), *"Je suis si contente de revenir mourir ici."*

Everyone in the village brought wine, eggs, butter, *poulet, confiture de sucre*—how everyone loved her. The carpenter's wife said, "The first time I saw her, and she smiled, I just had to go toward her like a little child."

The neighbors left and Georgette fell asleep. The cat, Moutzie, came and slept beside her on the bed. Then he left, before she woke. When we told her about it she looked very interested. *"Et qu'est ce qu'il a dit, Moutzie?"*

Late that night she looked straight at Monique and said, *"Quelle drame! Ma vie est finie, et j'avais encore tant de belles choses à faire."*

The next morning she said to Monique, *"J'ai peur."* She said it twice. She waited a little while and then said, *"Mon Dieu, me voulez-vous?"* She waited again, for almost an hour. Then she said, *"Je suis prête."*

As the days ran their course we shared with her the last two experiences through which she was to pass. The first was a tragedy of astonishment. *"Comment est-ce possible?"* she said on Saturday night—the end of her life had come and she could not believe it. But simultaneously with this drama she was living another—one which had the aspect of consciousness and which we were prepared to understand. Georgette herself had prepared us. In her book, writing of pneumonia and the approach of death, she had described every stage of her experience. "My days were not mine alone," she wrote, "I shared them with a succession of circles which opened to me on another plane." And now we watched what she had then likened to a "rehearsal of death"—her attempt "to follow that impossible following of one's mysterious passage." It duplicated exactly her written words. "I was engrossed above all by the great tasks which seemed to me urgent. With all the strength of my being I set myself to watch the core of my being. I did not want it to perish utterly. I worked to detach it from my body. I wanted to tear it out of myself and throw it to its new beginning, in order that the perils of the dying body should not reach it."

These words had not been "literature"—we now watched her live them in a drama which became objective in the great sense of the word. This was so clear to us that we didn't intrude into her "great effort to understand." We watched that effort as it absorbed her and we relinquished all personal longings for words of love and farewell. We understood that she "saw from very far away those she loved most," and we spoke to her only of our understanding.

Every time we used the word "understand" her peace seemed to increase. But once I didn't understand. I thought she would want to hear the Rachmaninoff and I put on the record in the next room. But she called to me. "No, *chérie*, *c'est* trop *beau*". . . .

She would not speak of her suffering except to say, *"Je n'ai pas le droit de m'apitoyer sur moi-même quand il y a tant de soldats qui souffrent et meurent pitolyablement."* During all these days she did not once, outwardly, leave the circle of serenity that had always ringed her outer and visible life. What she had lived that was invisible to the casual observer had been as grandly conceived as was her present encounter with death. The knowledge of this was what made it possible for us too to remain objective. Neither of us could allow the great conception to be marred. What literally broke my heart and at the same time kept me from giving way to my grief, was this proof of how deep the sense of form can go: not for art alone, but for life itself, and death—*that* deep, that strong, that true. She had always shown us how to live; now she was showing us how to die. This was all I could think about in those last days. And I knew I would never stop thinking about it.

The idea of her idea of death filled my mind so totally that I was not able to believe she was dying. It was as if we were merely discussing the fact of death and wondering, when that distant event came, how we were equipped to meet it. I went to the postoffice and sent cables to America, and to Jane in London, that the end was approaching; I remember standing at the *guichet*, writing these incredible words, and attaching no reality to them; I went back up the hill and resumed our life together as we had always lived it—an exaltation about *something*— about the very sense of life—that was now having its moment of eternity.

Every morning she said *"Bon jour"* to us, with a special accent on the *"bon."* It was in these short familiar phrases that our real farewells were said.

By Thursday she had begun to talk in symbols, and numbers, repeating over and over, *"Un, deux, trois, quatre,"* always emphasizing the *"quatre."* Sometimes she said, *"Moi, moi."* We knew she was talking of the octave, and the "I," according to Gurdjieff. And when she said to me very clearly, *"Tu sais, chérie, tu as toujours l'idée de trois, quatre, cinq, six—ce n'est pas bien,"* I knew exactly what she meant: "You must not go always too fast, you will lose much; you must begin at *do,* not *mi;* build from *do* to *mi,* then pass the half-tone to fa— consciously." I told her that I understood.

On Friday morning when we asked if she was suffering she said, *"Pas du corps."* All that day she was lucid, and that was the day she smiled so ineffably. Old friends and new ones came to see her. When we told her they were there tears filled her eyes, but without changing the serenity of her face. She received them as if she were not ill, with no trace of tears, saying *"Contente,"* *"Au revoir,"* giving her hand to be kissed. At least ten people saw her and her reception was like a conscious performance, holding everyone within the frame of the perfected picture.

An hour later she became obsessed with the idea that Gurdjieff was coming—*"Il vient, je le sais, il est déja là —il est entré par en bas."* Then she asked us to tell her the truth—was he there? We said that he was trying to come.

In the evening mail there was an inter-zone card from

Paris, with a message: that Gurdjieff had said she had
"*beaucoup de courage*" and called her "friend." With a
transfigured face she said, "*Il a dit cela?*" And then she
made her last statement: "*Alors . . . nous allons mourir
sans mourir?*"

Her new wound, at the base of the spine, became worse
every day, had to be dressed, gangrene was beginning; but
it was almost impossible to lift her out of bed. After five
minutes of gentle lifting, by all three of us, I would hold
her in my arms while the nurse worked quickly. Her whole
body beat like a strong heart.

Friday night it took almost ten minutes to lift her,
but she insisted. Monique and I held her, but she was unconscious. Back in bed, she looked at me and said, "*Tu
étais là aussi?*" Then she laughed and made a joke for
me: "*Ah, toi, tu ne rate jamais.*"

On Saturday morning she could no longer talk. Late
that night she said, distinctly, "*Comment est-ce possible?*"

On Sunday morning, when we asked if she was
hungry, she said, "*Mais . . . oui.*" What a communication
there was in the little pause between the two words; what
pathos in the childlike deprecation of the "*oui*"—as if she
were saying, "Yes, my body is still here, it is even hungry.
C'est curieux, n'est ce pas?"

All day Sunday she slept, with an extra *piqure* at
one o'clock when we feared she was suffering. The nurse
said, "She is dying, she cannot live through the night." I
was hearing other words—written words of Georgette's:
"My spirit will go away alone, without belongings, to begin

again with the seasons its human season." And I remembered other words that she had said, long ago: *"La jour de ma mort, il ne faut pas être triste, car ce sera un jour de fête pour mon âme."*

. . . She was sleeping. In the next room I was telling our neighbor how she sang *"Je tremble en voyant ton visage"* . . . how she presented the syllables, *"la niege,"* at the end . . . The nurse called, "Come quickly, she has opened her eyes." We reached her bed and held her to us. Her eyes were closing, she could not see. Her breathing was so soft and untroubled that we could scarcely hear it, but we knew at last that she was dying. Then, with no perceptible sign or sound or movement, she was dead. It was like a flower dying, or a leaf—as she wrote in her farewell to the Muette: "in a slow spiral, returning gently to the earth."

. . . It was half past eight and Georgette was dead.

I sat beside her until dawn. I held her right hand. I hadn't known whether death would be natural or terrifying. It was natural. I thought: I have never known anything that is strong until now; *nothing* that I can do will ever make Georgette smile again. Dawn came. I thought: thank you for your existence. I went into the next room and lay down. Monique was lying down in the room below. The light came from Georgette's door as it sometimes had in the last months—a signal that she had wakened and I could go in to see if she was suffering. I lay on my bed—she is not suffering now. I thought: I am going to sleep in a world where Georgette is not. For the first time in twenty-two years she is not with us. Soon she will be in a grave, near us ... *"ce petit âme mysterieux et silencieux."*

From Jane: At first I could not write at all—words seemed to be nothing, to have nothing to do with this. I was in town when your cable came. I had expected it but not feared it. You remember years ago, at the Prieuré, when Gurdjieff celebrated Georgette's "birthday." Well, I thought all day: this is another birthday, and I sent greetings for it: "Not farewell but fare forward, voyageur."

I read and re-read her last days as you tell them, and I think I know what she was trying to do and say. "As we go, so we come again." Georgette will never perish. Die we all must, but we can hope that none of us who has "eaten" of Gurdjieff's food will ever perish. Elspeth and I spent Sunday—the last day of Georgette's life—roaming in memory through all the lovely past in Paris, sharing images of all your rooms and costumes, hearing again voices and music and laughter. It was a delightful journey. At the end Elspeth said, "Oh, Georgette will always remain alive and living for me." How much more this must be true for you and Monique, when you are rested and can know her instant and present as she always was—if only in the heart's embrace.

THE EXTRA DAY

O*ctober, 1945, Hotel Brevoort, New York:* Washington Square is almost the same—October trees instead of May trees, a waterless fountain, a high apartment building where a beautiful house used to stand. I sit on a bench and wait for twilight and breathe in the smell of October leaves, slowly falling . . . *odeur du temps.* Lights begin to shine in windows. The white door of No. 47 is brighter than all the others—this is not my imagination, there is a fan of light over it that was not there before. The front of the building is made of false new bricks instead of the old ones, but does it matter? The door could open, now as then . . . It does open for me and Georgette comes out of it, smiling. She walks toward me. *Qui nous raconte qu'elle est morte?*

Through that door, in 1923, people went in to hear her sing, every night for sixty-two nights. Through that door, in May, we three came out and went to France. I remember, I remember, all that happened there. All this day I have lived in New York doing things I can't remem-

241

ber. My New York day has disappeared and in its place
I have lived our life again. I have had an extra day.

I shall always have it. Years will pass and with every
day I shall have this extra day. A war has come and gone,
wars will come and go, but my earthly story with a
heavenly meaning will go on for me forever. And is this
enough? It is so tempting to say yes, it is more than
enough. But this I must not say. I must live to its conclusion
a story we began together, in Fontainebleau, on our quest
to find our lives by losing them. Have I the strength to
begin again that struggle? I do not think so. I think "I
cannot" and I feel "I will." Can I find the courage, once
more, to go back and begin again that turning on an endless wheel? And for what? I am not quite clear. I only
know that out of gratitude for what I have had, I must go
and try again.

"What secret do these men bear with them to the tomb? Why are
they wondered at without being understood? Why are they ac-
quainted with things of which others know nothing? Why do they
conceal what all men burn to know?

"There is indeed a formidable secret . . . There is a science
and a force . . . There is one sole, universal and imperishable
doctrine, strong as the supreme reason, simple like all that is
great, intelligible like all that is universally and absolutely true.
This doctrine has been the parent of all others . . . The secret
constitutes the science of 'good and evil,' and the secret of indefi-
nite human progress is in that expression 'the kingdom of
heaven.' "

Giverny, Eure, France, 1949.